Loving
YOUR
WIFE
WELL

Also by Matt Jacobson

Loving

YOUR
WIFE
WELL

A 52-WEEK DEVOTIONAL
FOR THE DEEPER, RICHER MARRIAGE
YOU DESIRE

MATT JACOBSON

Revell

a division of Baker Publishing Group
Grand Rapids, Michigan

Published by Revell
a division of Baker Publishing Group
PO Box 6287, Grand Rapids, MI 49516-6287
www.revellbooks.com

Printed in the United States of America

Library of Congress Cataloging-in-Publication Data
Names: Jacobson, Matt, author.
Title: Loving your wife well : a 52-week devotional for the deeper, richer marriage you desire / Matt Jacobson.
Description: Grand Rapids, MI : Revell, a division of Baker Publishing Group, [2022]
Identifiers: LCCN 2022014197 | ISBN 9780800742416 (casebound) | ISBN 9780800736637 (paperback) | ISBN 9781493426713 (ebook)
Subjects: LCSH: Husbands—Religious life. | Marriage—Religious aspects— Christianity. | Man-woman relationships—Religious aspects—Christianity. | Wives—Psychology. | Devotional literature.
Classification: LCC BV4528.3 .J335 2022 | DDC 248.8/425—dc23/eng/20220524
LC record available at https://lccn.loc.gov/2022014197

Scripture quotations labeled CSB are from the Christian Standard Bible®, copyright © 2017 by Holman Bible Publishers. Used by permission. Christian Standard Bible® and CSB® are federally registered trademarks of Holman Bible Publishers.

Scripture quotations labeled ESV are from The Holy Bible, English Standard Version® (ESV®), copyright © 2001 by Crossway, a publishing ministry of Good News Publishers. Used by permission. All rights reserved. ESV Text Edition: 2016

Scripture quotations labeled KJV are from the King James Version of the Bible.

Scripture quotations labeled NASB are from the (NASB®) New American Standard Bible®, Copyright © 1960, 1971, 1977, 1995, 2020 by The Lockman Foundation. Used by permission. All rights reserved. www.lockman.org

Scripture quotations labeled NKJV are from the New King James Version®. Copyright © 1982 by Thomas Nelson. Used by permission. All rights reserved.

Scripture quotations labeled RSV are from the Revised Standard Version of the Bible, copyright 1946, 1952 [2nd edition, 1971] National Council of the Churches of Christ in the United States of America. Used by permission. All rights reserved worldwide.

The quotation by Eusebius on page 107 is from Michael Haverkamp, "The Scourging at the Pillar," Build on Rock, March 19, 2019, https://www.buildonrock.org/posts/the-scourging-at-the-pillar/.

Italics in Scripture quotations reflect the author's emphasis.

Baker Publishing Group publications use paper produced from sustainable forestry practices and post-consumer waste whenever possible.

22 23 24 25 26 27 28   7 6 5 4 3 2 1

To my lovely, biblical wife,
who walks in beauty.

—M

Contents

Contents

Contents

Introduction

Friend, your marriage is the most important relationship you will ever have this side of heaven. No aspect of your life will be left untouched by the woman you spend your life with. As husbands, sometimes we forget how the choices we make in our everyday interactions with our wife can impact our marriage. It's easy to lose sight of the spiritual importance and power of our relationship. That's why I want to share this book with you. The biblical truths and principles in this devotional have been the bedrock of my marriage to Lisa, and I know they will bless your marriage greatly too.

All the devotions in this book have the same format. Each week focuses on a single subject and includes a Scripture selection, followed by an exploration of the topic. Then there are a few questions for self-reflection and several practical suggestions for how you can apply the principles to your marriage over the coming week. Finally, each devotional reading ends with a sample prayer to help focus your thoughts.

Before you get started, keep in mind that *Loving Your Wife Well* can be read and applied by itself, but it was created as a companion devotional to *Loving Your Husband Well*, a book written by my wife, Lisa, for your wife.

Both devotionals follow a similar format, but the content in the devotional designed for wives is different because Lisa is writing to your wife on these topics from her perspective, and I write directly to you from mine . . . and, no, we didn't compare notes during the writing process!

Again, the devotionals can be read and applied independently, but when you and your wife are going through the same topics and Scriptures (though Lisa and I do use different translations at times), it makes for great discussion throughout the week and the opportunity to grow even closer together.

Maybe you're one of those men who remain very consistent in their devotional lives. But if it's not a regular part of your spiritual life and this process is new to you, I'd like to share with you some of my own personal practices for entering into devotional time with the Lord (when I'm vigilant and on my game!).

Here are the things I do:

Be consistent. Pick a specific day and time each week for devotional readings. Monday morning is a good time to begin this *weekly* devotional.

Avoid looking at my phone or computer. I've found it very beneficial not to even look at my phone or open my computer prior to my time meeting with God in the morning. Once in the digital world, it's difficult to get my focus back on the Lord and His Word, so I don't even go there.

Remember Whom I'm meeting with. I remind myself that I have the massive privilege to meet with the God of creation, the God of Abraham, Isaac, and Jacob, the God of all history, and I prostrate myself before Him— face to the ground—and worship Him. He is worthy.

Seek the Father's guidance. I pray that He will help me hear His voice through His Word and in my reading, and that He will do His work in my heart for His purposes in my life.

Take the time to read and ponder, think about, and/or meditate on the Scripture reading. I think about what I've read and seek to hear the voice of the Spirit. What is it that God is seeking to teach me today?

Pray. I give thanks (never forget to give thanks) and pray about burdens, concerns, and needs, asking for God's perspective, favor, and protection.

Lift my thoughts in praise. I like to listen to an upbeat praise song or a hymn that reminds me of the power of my God and His goodness.

If you're reading this devotional along with your wife or by yourself, choose a specific day of the week and a regular time, and stick with it! Read through the devotion and use the rest of the week to think about and apply the principles and suggestions to your own life and relationship with your wife. And if you're doing them together, be sure to take the lead on finding a time when the two of you can come together to discuss the week's topic and ways that you can grow together in Christlikeness and be a blessing to each other.

Welcome to the journey of seeking to love your wife well. The fruit of this journey in Lisa's and my life has been sweet. May God bless you and your wife in the coming year.

1

Love

Beloved, let us love one another, for love is of God; and everyone who loves is born of God and knows God. He who does not love does not know God, for God is love.

1 John 4:7–8 NKJV

When asked, "Do you truly love your wife?" a quick response typically follows: "Of course! Yes, I love my wife." We usually have a general idea of what we mean, but is our idea of loving her the same as what God means when He instructs us to love each other?

Love has many expressions, and there are several kinds of love. But the kind of love God wants you to have for your wife goes far beyond those warm feelings you get on a starry summer night when all is well between the two of you. Any husband can choose to be romantic. But who gives the kind of love the

Holy Spirit speaks of in 1 John, where we are told simply to love one another?

If we dig just a little, we see that the writer is speaking of a specific kind of love. This is the love that is from God, that comes without conditions and causes us to sacrifice ourselves for the object of our love. So, the question again: Do you selflessly love and readily sacrifice yourself for your wife?

When your wife gives you what you desire and pleases you with her words and actions, it's easy to respond in kind and loving ways. It's the natural thing to do.

But in 1 John, God is requiring something far more, something completely *unnatural* to the typical way of thinking. He's asking you to love (your wife) with a different kind of love—a love that costs and is given without the expectation or the requirement of reciprocation. You might call it "Calvary love"— the kind of love Jesus Christ demonstrated on the cross. He gave His life for us while we were still in our sins. We merited nothing, but He still gave. And this is the same love God is calling you to give . . . to your wife.

Is your heart, right now, filled with this love for her? Do you love her without condition? Are you ready and willing—even eager—to lay down your life for her, sacrificing yourself in practical ways, as you seek what is truly best for her? Or do you find yourself thinking, *I'll love her if . . .* ?

To love as God loves can seem like an absurd ask, but your Father will never require of you what He has not made provision for. When He asks you to do something, He has already ensured you have what you need to be successful. So you don't have to guess or search to have a love like that for your wife. First John says this love is from God. He gave it to you. The person who is "born of God" has received God's love, and it is there for a purpose—to give away, every day, pouring into the lives of others, starting with your wife's heart.

But this instruction to love comes with a warning: Loving your wife this way isn't merely an option you can choose as a Christian husband. The Bible indicates that loving (her) this way is evidence of someone who is "born of God" and who "knows God." And if you don't love this way, the Scripture warns that *you don't know God.*

This different kind of love, *agapē* love in the Greek, isn't just what God does. Agapē love is who God is—God is love—and God says it is who you are, too, if you are born of Him. Can you now see that loving your wife well is principally about your relationship with God? It's the first place to look when seeking to love your wife well. God's love in you will overthrow the natural inclinations of your flesh and bring a revolution in how you see and interact with your wife.

If you find your love running thin or low, turn your heart to the Father, draw near to Him right now, and ask Him to fill you with His selfless, agapē love for your wife in the coming week.

Reflection

- Am I filled with a selfless, sacrificial, unconditional love for my wife?
- Am I ready to lay down my life for her today?
- Am I willing to sacrifice my desires to serve her without expectation of repayment?
- What does loving my wife look like in the coming week?

Application

When it comes to loving your wife in meaningful ways, there is no one-size-fits-all answer. But setting aside time to think about God's call on your life with regard to her will help focus your thoughts on your unique relationship.

The doing starts with self-reflection and a focus on her genuine needs, continues in clarifying conversation, and culminates in action.

Prayer

God my Father, consistently loving as You call me to love seems impossible. Yet I know You indwell me with Your Spirit and have empowered me to live in obedience to the instruction in Your Word. Please show me where selfishness and self-focus are hiding in my heart so that I can identify them, repent of them, and mature in my character and faith. Help me this day to truly and selflessly love my wife. And help me to be motivated by obedience to You and not by what I want in return from her. I pray that I would be a blessing to her. May she experience Your love through how I love and serve her this week. In Jesus's name, amen.

2

Priority

For this reason a man shall leave his father and mother and be joined to his wife, and the two shall become one flesh.

Ephesians 5:31 RSV

We all know how to answer questions about our priorities. Is God a priority in your life? "Yes!" Is your wife a priority in your life? "Absolutely!" But the truth about our real priorities is found not in the right words but in how we spend our time.

What are you pursuing this week, this month, this season of life? Why is this an important question for a husband? Because what you pursue with your time is what you treasure in your heart, and everyone knows it, especially your wife. However busy we may be, one fact remains: We always have time for our *real* priorities, and everyone gives their heart (their time) to what they treasure.

You would never say that your job, sports, your hobby, your man friends, the kids, or even the ministry you're committed to at the local church are priorities over your wife, would you? No, of course you wouldn't *say* any of those things. But what is your time and attention saying about your priorities over the last month?

As Christian men, we're quick to say that God and His instruction in the Word are our priority, but if that is to be true of us in practical terms—in daily life—we must embrace how He has defined us and what He has identified as our priorities. The One who paid for your soul defines who you are and what your priorities must be. He has been very clear about this matter as it relates to marriage.

In bringing you and your wife together, God established a fundamental change in your identity. Your marriage is what He is doing in the world—not merely what you decided to do. From the beginning, God declared that in marriage a man and wife are no longer two separate, independent people. Where there were two distinct entities, there is now only one. "Therefore shall a man leave his father and his mother, and shall cleave unto his wife: and they shall be one flesh" (Gen. 2:24 KJV).

This declaration is about far more than sex and the children that are the physical embodiment of that kind of oneness. If that's all it meant, leaving the parents wouldn't have been mentioned. Biblical oneness is physical, but it's also emotional and spiritual. No longer two separate people who used to have healthy (or otherwise) entanglements and commitments to others, you are now a new, single unit composed of each other. Does this mean that your individuality is forever lost?

No. Certainly, you remain individuals. But it does mean that your independence and independent purpose are now past. It is forevermore "we" and no longer "I." Living out that unity of oneness makes your wife, after God, your first priority.

When the Father truly has His rightful place in your life, His Spirit will clarify the understanding, strengthen the commitment, and bring vigor to the pursuit of biblical unity with your wife. When you embrace God's declaration of who you are in marriage, your wife will never have to question her position in your heart. She'll never have to compete with other people or things. She will know, and experience, that she is a treasured woman—just as God intended. The husband who is yielded to God makes his wife his first priority.

Reflection

Ask your wife these questions:

- When you think about how I spend my time, what would you say are my top three priorities?
- Do you feel like you are my number-one priority in this world?
- From your perspective, is there anything I can do to enhance the oneness of our marriage?
- What could I do this week that would give you the comfort of knowing you are in first place (after God!) in my heart?

Application

Think through the coming week and identify specific ways to address the things your wife mentions in your discussion with her.

Be specific and select a day and time when you will implement those changes.

Make sure your wife doesn't feel as if she is at the bottom of your priority list this week.

Prayer

God my Father, I desire to see myself as You see me. Help me to grow in my understanding of our marriage as one of oneness and unity. By bringing us together in marriage and declaring that we are one, You have established that my wife is my principal priority. Help me to follow through in practical ways with living out that truth. Give me increasing understanding of my wife and help me value her by protecting the unity of our marriage as other priorities keep pressing in on our relationship. Thank You, Lord. In Jesus's name, amen.

3

Faith

But without faith it is impossible to please him: for he that cometh to God must believe that he is, and that he is a rewarder of them that diligently seek him.

Hebrews 11:6 KJV

Are you a man of faith?

There will come a day when many people within the church will discover that they were not people of faith, despite their strong declarations and their identification with Christian things.

Speaking of these people, Jesus said,

Not everyone that saith unto me, Lord, Lord, shall enter into the kingdom of heaven; but he that doeth the will of my Father which is in heaven. Many will say to me in that day, Lord, Lord, have we not prophesied in thy name? and in thy name have cast out devils? and in thy name done many wonderful works? And then will I profess unto them, I never knew you: depart from me, ye that work iniquity. Therefore whosoever heareth these sayings of mine, and doeth them, I will liken him unto a wise man, which built his house upon a rock. (Matt. 7:21–24 KJV)

These words of Jesus are chilling and sobering. How can you know if you are a man of faith? First, you must be proactive. There are no casual Christians in the church of Jesus Christ. Simply calling oneself "Christian" in no way establishes whether it is true or not. It's your job to examine yourself. Second Corinthians 13:5 says, "Examine yourselves, whether ye be in the faith" (KJV).

The people Jesus spoke of had been certain they were "in the faith" and were shocked to discover they were not. But even if you examine yourself, how can you know?

The comforting truth is that you can know with certainty, but it will be based on God's terms, not your own ideas of what it means to be a true disciple of Jesus.

First John 5:13 says, "These things have I written unto you that believe on the name of the Son of God; that ye may know that ye have eternal life, and that ye may believe on the name of the Son of God" (KJV).

Many are too casual about the word *believe*. It carries with it a meaning far deeper than the simple declaration, "I believe." To believe on God's terms—to have saving faith—is to recognize that without the righteousness of Jesus Christ, you are condemned before God as a lawbreaker. You must repent of your sins and receive the free gift of God's mercy and grace through the death, burial, and resurrection of Jesus Christ and believe that His shed blood paid the penalty for the guilt and shame of your sin. This saving faith brings you to the conviction that all God says is true and will come to pass and that you, now empowered by the Spirit of God who indwells you, will order your life according to the instruction found in God's Word, the Bible.

Without faith it is impossible to please God. This is what it means to believe—to have the conviction of saving faith.

If one desires to know what it means to be a man of faith, Hebrews 11 is a great place to start. Often called the "Hall of Faith," it recounts the stories of the many faithful believers who have gone before. And what is clearly seen throughout is that the man of true faith is serious to the bone and has given his life to God.

God trifles with no one, and no one should presume to trifle with God. To be a Christian husband is to be a man of faith whose testimony would fit into Hebrews 11. You have the sacred charge of bearing that faith in all aspects of leading humbly in your marriage. It's the journey of maturity God is calling you to.

Reflection

- What is the depth of my commitment to faith in the shed blood of Jesus Christ, the Son of God?
- Have I truly been reconciled to the Father? Am I in fellowship with Him?

Application

- Examine yourself. Are you in the faith?
- Read the above Scriptures with your wife.
- Commit yourself to the Father, through Jesus Christ, for growth and deeper commitment in true, saving faith.
- If you already have a deep, serious faith and are confident in your salvation, rejoice with your wife and give thanks to God.

Prayer

God my Father, when I take time to read Jesus's words to all those people who were confident of their standing with Him—"I never knew you: depart from me"(Matt. 7:23 KJV)—I want no part of casual, nonserious faith that leads only to destruction. Lord, I believe, and I pray that I will grow deep in my faith and become the godly, biblical husband You intend me to be. I worship You and believe in the gift of Your grace that You give to all who repent. Thank You for Your way of salvation provided through the sacrifice of Jesus Christ, Your Son. Here is my life. It is Yours for Your glory. In Jesus's name, amen.

4

Healing

> He heals the brokenhearted
> and binds up their wounds.
>
> Psalm 147:3 NASB

Every one of us needs healing because every one of us is broken in some way, including you and your wife. You fell in love and pursued marriage with love for each other, but you arrived at your wedding day with more than love.

Certainly, you brought to that celebration all your great qualities, spiritual gifts, and best intentions for each other. But you also brought all the negative, destructive, hurtful experiences you've had as a result of your past sinful choices or the sinful choices of others. The power they exercised on your heart and mind went into who you both were on the day of your marriage and are a part of who each of you is today.

No one has avoided the cold, destructive grasp of sin. Maybe it was a choice you or your wife made. Maybe it was a wicked choice someone else made that damaged you somewhere in the secret places of your heart. Whatever the circumstances, sin mars, maims, and disfigures and brings with it regret. *Oh, how I wish "that" had never happened.*

Your Father in heaven knows about wounds, bruises, and brokenness—what has touched you and your wife. He knows well all the flawed and injured places in your hearts. That's why God sent His Son to be wounded and bruised, the flesh of His face and body torn apart. His crucifixion followed; spikes were nailed securely through the bones of His wrists and feet, deep into wood to lift Him up, totally naked, to public shame and ridicule.

Sin inflicts wounds, breaks hearts, and leaves regret, but it does not go unanswered.

> But he was wounded for our transgressions, he was bruised for our iniquities: the chastisement of our peace was upon him; and with his stripes we are healed. (Isa. 53:5 KJV)

As Jesus Christ paid the price for your guilt that you might be healed and your relationship with God your Father be reconciled, He also paid the price for the sins others have committed against you and your wife—those who purposefully, or unknowingly, inflicted deep wounds on your hearts.

Unhealed wounds and hearts that remain broken exercise a great deal of power in marriage. God doesn't want these wounds left unattended. He came to heal them, to sanctify them, to turn Satan's intentions for these wounded, hidden places on their heads so that what your Enemy meant for evil, God can use for good. It may seem impossible that good could ever come from that cesspool, that ash heap, but as we read in Romans 8:28, the Father will work "all things" together for good. Not just the best things that have happened to you and your wife but *all things*, even the worst things that have touched your souls and disfigured your hearts.

What is true is not what we feel, but what God has said.

Are you willing to believe what the Bible says about these things? That God can miraculously use them for good? The wounds and regrets you both brought into your marriage can be healed only by God, who waits patiently, desiring that you choose faith and trust Him with your deepest pain and brokenness.

Have you or your wife been hurt, betrayed, spoken ill of, or heartbroken by your own sin or the sins of others? Many husbands and wives have received salvation but continue to hold on to wounds long into their marriage. Kept in your hands, these wounds can never heal. And only you can give your wounds to the Father, but as all-powerful as He is, God will never take from you what you will not surrender to Him.

And you cannot lead where you have not walked.

God gave your wife to you so you could care for the deep places of her heart where life's wounds have broken things desperately in need of grace. Remind yourself that the wounded tend to wound those closest to them. Where you both are weak, where each of you is vulnerable, where you both are insecure because of regrets from past sin—all manifest in behaviors that negatively impact your marriage. But God has entrusted to you this position as a husband because He desires to minister His grace in these very areas to your wife through you.

This requires your honesty with each other to name those areas, grieve and cry over them together, forgive where it is required, and give them to the Father, thanking Him for His mercy and for His grace. Then, when the Enemy desires to use pain or regret on your heart like an ice pick, reject that incoming attack in the name of Jesus. Refuse the offer from the Tempter to take back what you have given to your loving, forgiving Father.

Reflection

- Am I a member of the walking wounded—continuing to function without allowing God's healing touch in my life?
- Is my wife living with deep wounds that have never been healed?
- How have these things been impacting our communication?
- Do I believe the Word? Am I willing to trust, to have faith, to allow God to heal these wounds and miraculously use them for a good I cannot see right now?

Application

Discuss with your wife any woundedness that you are carrying and ask her about the wounds she feels she still carries.

When your wife is responding to you or a circumstance in your marriage from her woundedness (in a way that may be very hurtful to you), don't take the bait. Your Enemy wants to use this as a wedge between the two of you. Anticipate and recognize this and respond softly with words of grace—the grace you have received from the Father through the sacrifice of Jesus Christ.

Remind yourself that, today and always, God intends for you to be a channel of His grace to your wife.

You both may need a godly, wise, biblical, Spirit-gifted counselor to help work through some of these things.

Prayer

God my Father, I know You are the Healer. I know that this healing was provided by the torture, death, and resurrection of Jesus Christ. Even so, many things that have happened to my wife and me rise from our past and have power I know You don't want them to have. I desire to listen only to Your voice of truth. Lord God, please take from me the wounds of my life. I release them to You for the healing only You can provide. Please remove their power from my mind. Please help me to be a minister of Your grace to my wife today. I also pray that she, too, would release the grip on her wounds and regrets and that we both may trust You to use them according to your promise in Romans 8:28, bringing something good out of what can only remain broken in our hands. I love You, my God, my King, and my Father—who loves me with a love that will not fail. May my life be a channel of blessing to my wife and others this day. In Jesus's name, amen.

5

Affirmation

Let every one of us please his neighbour for his good to edification.

Romans 15:2 KJV

Does your wife often feel like a wilted flower placed too close to a south-facing window in the summer? Many do. If your wife never does, you're to be commended. A husband's sincere words of love and affirmation are to his wife's heart what fresh water is to a dry plant.

The wife of a Christian husband should never have to spend weeks, months, or years without hearing from him the value of her contribution to their marriage, home, community, and world.

You may have an ocean of deep gratitude, value, and respect for your wife, but left unexpressed, it does literally no good.

Your wife isn't a mind reader. She cannot intuitively experience all the kind, affirming thoughts toward her that remain your private opinion. She needs to hear regularly from you what it is about her you love, appreciate, value, like, desire, respect, and are impressed with.

A man may be quick to praise his wife to others but rarely, if ever, speak a word of encouragement or affirmation directly to her. It may make others think she's a wonderful woman, but what does it make her think? Nothing! And, she'll never know unless you tell her.

The voices tearing down your wife come from every direction. Regardless of how intelligent, competent, hardworking, loving, and creative she may be, just about every wife at some point feels she's falling behind, is a failure, and will never measure up. And why wouldn't she feel this way? There's not much in society that affirms the value and worth of a wife; in fact, it's quite the opposite.

Our culture is filled with the deceitful voice of the Enemy of your wife's soul, seeking to discourage and tear her down. It tells her every day in every media that she's not enough: She's not pretty enough, slim enough, valuable enough, smart enough. And she's not only not enough . . . she'll *never* be enough.

You are your wife's indispensable voice to counteract all the negative input she gets from every possible place. Are you using the power of the voice God gave you to speak affirming words into your wife's heart every day? She doesn't just *want* to hear your words of encouragement; she *needs* to hear them.

The emotional health of your wife's heart is like a finite pitcher of fresh, pure water pouring out into the lives of you and everyone in her world. Even if she's doing tasks she loves to bless you with, she's still pouring out of a finite vessel.

Who will pour into her?

You play a vital role in your wife's emotional health by how you pour your love, encouragement, and affirmation into her. God's Word tells us to build each other up, and when you embrace this crucial ministry in your wife's life, that pitcher of love and giving will pour out all over you.

Embrace the instruction of Scripture and what every husband who regularly cherishes and affirms his wife has learned: He who loves, cherishes, and regularly affirms his wife soon discovers that she gives back to him more than he ever poured into her soul.

Reflection

- Have I been affirming my wife with words of encouragement?
- How does her spirit in the home seem this week? Is she lighthearted and buoyant, or is she discouraged and in need of more regular, strong words of praise, affirmation, and acknowledgment of her great value?

Application

Each morning when your wife is fully awake, embrace her and tell her how much you love her.

At some point in the day, text her and tell her that you are thinking about her and deeply appreciate her because . . . (you fill in the blank!).

When you see each other at night, find something to praise her for.

Remind yourself that you are using the truth of who she truly is to remind her of how much you love, admire, respect, and appreciate her. You're filling that pitcher because God placed you in her life for that very purpose.

Prayer

God my Father, thank You for giving me such a beautiful, wonderful wife. She is truly a gift from Your hand. Help me to be sure to express this to her regularly. Help me to be consistent in affirming her for the many excellent qualities she has. Remind me that I need to pour into the pitcher of her heart so she can continue to love me and others from a reservoir that is regularly filled. May I cherish her with Your love this week. In Jesus's name, amen.

6

Spiritual Warfare

Finally, my brethren, be strong in the Lord, and in the power of his might. Put on the whole armour of God, that ye may be able to stand against the wiles of the devil. For we wrestle not against flesh and blood, but against principalities, against powers, against the rulers of the darkness of this world, against spiritual wickedness in high places.

Ephesians 6:10–12 KJV

The sun may shine clear and hot, but a war zone is a terrible place for sunbathing. No wise commander would remove his fatigues, take the clip out of his rifle, set his helmet aside, slather up with suntan lotion, and stretch out. That man would be a fool to ignore the context of his existence—to ignore reality. He wouldn't need anybody to tell him, "You're in a war zone, soldier. Stay frosty!"

What is your mental state regarding the war zone you're living in? Are you living with that same intensity, that same focus, that same alertness to the reality of your spiritual life? And what is that reality? You're in a war zone! It may not feel like it when you're at work closing the latest deal, at the coast on vacation, out for dinner with your wife, or doing chores around the house with the kids. How you happen to be feeling in the moment doesn't change the reality of what you are surrounded by, according to the Word.

Unlike US troops deployed in war zones, you need to be reminded of the war zone you're in because of the comfort, culture noise, and distractions of life here on Earth. Exactly how is this war zone of your life described in the Bible? What or whom are you fighting? Where is this war taking place? The book of Ephesians says you're fighting "against principalities, against powers, against the rulers of the darkness of this world" (6:12 KJV). You're fighting "spiritual wickedness in high places" (v. 12 KJV).

It reads like a line out of a fantasy novel, doesn't it? But it's straight from the Bible—a clear explanation of what you're up against every day.

So, which will it be? Prep for that suntan, or serious, resolute focus? We know the fate of the casual soldier in the war zone. It's the same fate as that of many Christian men going through the spiritual war zone of their lives with little thought of the battle they're in.

You and your wife are heading into this spiritual battle zone every day. The Word says you are responsible for how you are leading. Are you leading well? What are you doing to prepare for the rulers of the darkness of this world, for the spiritual wickedness in high places you surely will encounter?

God has provided an answer: He expects you to dress yourself for battle. Ephesians 6:13–18 (KJV) says,

> Wherefore take unto you the whole armour of God, that ye may be able to withstand in the evil day, and having done all, to stand. Stand therefore, having your loins girt about with truth, and having on the breastplate of righteousness; and your feet shod with the preparation of the gospel of peace; Above all, taking the shield of faith, wherewith ye shall be able to quench all the fiery darts of the wicked. And take the helmet of salvation, and the sword of the Spirit, which is the word of God: Praying always with all prayer and supplication in the Spirit, and watching thereunto with all perseverance and supplication for all saints.

The apostle Paul is describing the war preparation of a Roman soldier and using that analogy to speak of the spiritual preparations and disciplines necessary to wage a successful campaign in the Spirit on any given day. What's striking here is that while God provides the armor, in the space of three verses He tells the Christian to get dressed two times. He expects you to take the initiative to prepare for battle.

When it comes to your war every day as a Christian man, particularly regarding your marriage, Satan has you in his crosshairs. He's playing for keeps and intends to take you—and your marriage—out. God gives you a heads-up on where the Enemy operates, brings you what you need for success, then says, "Get dressed."

Prepare yourself for battle—today and every day. Stay frosty.

Reflection

- Have I truly embraced the reality of the spiritual war zone of my life?
- Do I really believe I'm headed into battle, where I'm surrounded by a deadly Enemy, every day?
- Am I leading my wife well, praying over her and with her about the spiritual threats everywhere around us?
- Am I remembering that, as God's son, I am more than a conqueror through His power when I'm obedient, when I do what God tells me in His Word to do?

Application

Do battle prep at the beginning of every day:

- Pray for yourself, for your alertness and focus.
- Pray for and with your wife.
- Read the Word every day.
- Remain confident that you serve the God who laughs at His enemies, but don't forget the responsibility He gives you to "get dressed" for success in a firefight.

Prayer

God my Father, You have identified me in Your Word as one who is a warrior in the midst of a battle. Lord, help me to keep this reality in mind at all times. There are so many distractions to take my focus off this truth—distractions that diminish my resolve and cause me to stumble. I know my Enemy wants to destroy me and my marriage. I know my wife and I are a target. May I be vigilant this week, and may that focus start with walking closely with You, listening to Your voice through Your Word, and praying. Lord, may I fight well this week as I draw near to You. In Jesus's name, amen.

7

Laughter

There is . . . a time to laugh . . . and a time to dance.

Ecclesiastes 3:1, 4 KJV

Does God want you to laugh, celebrate, and be happy? It's often heard in religious circles that God doesn't want you to be happy; He wants you to be holy. Others say that happiness is the world's counterfeit for the joy of the Lord. Those statements might have a pious ring to them, but they don't fit too well into the full scope of the Bible, including the wedding in Cana, where Jesus made sure there was more than enough wine to keep the party going long into the night (John 2:1–12).

Such declarations are also out of step with the many times the Bible says, "Blessed is the man . . ." or "blessed are they . . ." or "blessed is he . . ." *Blessed* in these multiple uses simply means "happy."

They don't fit well into the book of Ecclesiastes either, which states, there is a time for everything—including a time for dancing and a time for laughter. As it turns out, happiness is God's idea.

Some men are naturally upbeat and positive and can see the sun through the blackest clouds. It's a personality trait that stands them in good stead on difficult days. If that's you, you naturally bring a positive spirit into your marriage relationship—as you should. If you're not of this personality, or if life has managed to squeeze the happiness out of you, it's important to understand the effect you have on your wife when you're less than positive.

The power of your presence will find its way into every part of your home—and your wife's heart. It's good to reflect on who you are in your home because your countenance and spirit wield real power and influence. You are a compelling presence. Regardless of what you think about yourself, the spirit you exude forcefully affects everyone in your home, starting with your wife.

How natural and easy it is to focus on your feelings—anger, pressure, frustration, heaviness, concern, negativity—as your present reality rather than seeing those feelings for what they really are: a choice you are making. There's enough pressure in life to squeeze the lightness and fun out of everything. But you're not powerless. Your attitude is your choice, and you have a responsibility to care for the heart of the woman God has blessed you with. You're leading, and for others, you're setting the tone in your home.

With all you bring when you enter a room, the Bible says don't forget the times when it's appropriate to laugh and dance. It also says, "Rejoice in the Lord *always*: and again I say, Rejoice" (Phil. 4:4 KJV). This is about choosing a perspective, regardless of circumstances, and making sure that rejoicing—being exceedingly glad, positive, and grateful to God—is the baseline of who you are.

It's not about pretending everything is great when it isn't. False positives never last, and that same passage in Ecclesiastes does say there is a time to mourn. But, as a son of the Most High God, you are not to live as low and downcast. You're the husband. You're leading and impacting your wife. God is good, and there's much to be thankful for. Where your focus is, your mood and countenance will soon follow.

Reflection

- When I walk into a room, does my wife experience a positive spirit coming from me?
- Do I take time to relax and laugh and enjoy our life together in the everyday interactions between us?
- Do I have a habit of making excuses for a negative, downcast spirit rather than disciplining my mind to focus on God, His goodness, and His plans for us?
- Am I remembering that I am impacting all those around me by the spirit and attitude I exude?

Application

Recognize the very real power you exercise in your marriage by the lightness or heaviness of your spirit. Receive the admonition to rejoice always. When you're entering the home or transitioning to "together" time, take a moment to assess your spirit and countenance and choose to be positive.

What makes you laugh? Make a list of things that you find funny: funny moments, coincidences, or each other's antics that you've had a good laugh about over the years.

When you're tempted to go into a negative slump, remind yourself that you are instructed to rejoice—that this is a choice you are called to make.

Prayer

God my Father, Your Word is clear regarding how I am to live—with a positive, rejoicing, thankful spirit. And I see now that this is my responsibility—not something You will force upon me but something You tell me to choose. Help me to remember that my choice of attitude and spirit has a major impact on my wife and our home and that it also impacts my testimony as a follower of Jesus Christ. Thank You for telling us in Your Word that there is a time to laugh . . . and for Jesus's first miracle, making all that wine at the wedding in Cana! Lord, I want to be Your man. When I'm tempted to be negative, downcast, or pressured this week, help me to focus on the countless things I have to rejoice over, starting with the fact that You are God Almighty, who has blessed me and loved me and with whom I have a sure future in this life and for eternity. In Jesus's name, amen.

8

Trust

Trust in the LORD with all your heart,
and do not lean on your own understanding.
In all your ways acknowledge him,
and he will make straight your paths.

Proverbs 3:5–6 ESV

We grow in maturity when we discover, then embrace, the fact that God won't bargain with us. Even so, we can be a lot like Job, who was eager, even defiant, to remind God of his commitment, piety, and devotion when an endless list of bad things happened to him. Job had a point. By any logic under heaven, it wasn't fair. Job led a good life, was devoted to God, and still was crushed by one bitter trial after another.

But when God deals with us, He doesn't use our logic. He uses His own logic. And in the last few chapters of the book of Job, God emphasizes over everything else the one thing He wants from Job: trust.

> Where were you when I laid the foundations of the
> earth?
> Tell Me, if you have understanding.
> Who determined its measurements?
> Surely you know! . . .
> To what were its foundations fastened?
> Or who laid its cornerstone,
> When the morning stars sang together,
> And all the sons of God shouted for joy? . . .
>
> Have you commanded the morning since your days
> began,
> And caused the dawn to know its place. (Job 38:4–7, 12
> NKJV)

"Uh . . . no. I wasn't there, and I've never done that." Sometimes it's best just to be silent.

God is calling you to complete, unequivocal trust in Him regarding your present circumstances and your future prospects. He expects us to look past our circumstances to who He is and to have total confidence in what He is doing, regardless of how it feels in the moment, regardless of what you may or may not understand. It's as if God is saying to Job and everyone else, *I am the Creator. Look at the vastness, wonder, order, precision, and power of what I have created, and never stop trusting Me. Your best interests, biggest fears, deepest concerns, and brightest hopes are safe and secure in My hand.*

Because God is the perfect, loving heavenly Father, your trust in Him will never be betrayed, unvalued, diminished, or dangerous to your best interests. The storms of this life will rage on, but there's real peace and comfort in that level of confidence.

Trust in marriage can be beautiful and bring security too, but it's also very different from the trust you place in your perfect Father God. In human relationships, trust is risky because when trust is given, power is relinquished to an imperfect person. To trust is to choose to be vulnerable and exposed to the person you've just given the power to hurt you.

In your marriage, you are the object of that level of trust and risk. It might be countered that a husband is in the same position regarding putting his trust in his wife, and to a degree this is true. But a husband bears a greater responsibility before God for the relationship than a wife does. First Corinthians 11 says the head of Christ is God, the head of man is Christ, and the head of the woman is the man. The modern ear may chafe at this chain of authority, but what we focus on in this short passage is the Christian husband's grave responsibility, for which he will be held accountable before God, to love and lead his wife well. Such a relationship cannot thrive without trust, which must be reinforced and deepened throughout marriage.

God is worthy of your trust and will never hurt you, leave you, or forsake you. Your wife has chosen to be vulnerable and exposed to you. When she said "I do" on your wedding day, all her hopes and dreams were placed in your hands. She trusted you with the power to hurt her. Can your heavenly Father trust you to be worthy of your wife's trust in the weeks and months ahead? Can her heart safely trust in you?

Reflection

- Am I placing my whole trust in God, for everything?
- Am I an example of faith in God for my wife to see, even when things go wrong and adverse circumstances invade our lives?
- Have I lived in a manner that increases my wife's trust in me as a godly husband?

Application

Think about the last time you went through a difficult time. Did you go through that challenge with a settled confidence in God, or did it shake your faith? Ask for your wife's assessment of your leadership during that time.

Ask your wife to discuss her level of trust in you, but don't be negative or express disapproval if her answers are less than you'd hoped. Discuss barriers to her trust in you. If any, identify and purpose to change them.

If you've damaged her trust in a severe way, of course repenting and asking God and her to forgive you are in order. Restoring trust takes time, and you have no right to demand instant change or to be impatient with her. The only way to change the reputation you have with her is to be consistent over time as you draw near to God.

Prayer

God my Father, it's so easy for me to read in the Bible about the level of trust You're looking for from Your children without engaging at a heart level with how You desire for me to change. I don't want to be that man. I pray that I would grow and mature in this matter of trusting You in all circumstances and situations. And, Lord, I pray that I would be a man worthy of my wife's trust. Where I have compromised her trust, please restore those places in her heart. Please do Your work in me as I seek to honor her and You in being the husband worthy of her trust for Your glory. In Jesus's name, amen.

9

Joy

Now may the God of hope fill you with all joy and peace in believing, that you may abound in hope by the power of the Holy Spirit.

Romans 15:13 NKJV

Most men think about being joyful as much as they think about their next root canal. At first glance, it's not really a "guy" word, but God wants you to take more than a passing glance at this most important aspect of being a faithful husband.

Every day, you are in a position to have a powerful impact on your wife. What are you carrying into the house when you arrive? What do you allow to "live" with you? The weight of the world? The problems in the economy, politics, the unrest in society, frustrations at work, the next deal that you're putting together or that's falling apart, repairs that are needed around the house or on the car?

The spirit of your home and the lightness of your wife's heart come in large part from you. Your wife absorbs the essence of what you communicate—verbal and nonverbal. As a result, you have a great opportunity for the kind of home you establish through your spirit, demeanor, behavior, speech, and outlook.

What will it be in the coming week? A spirit of heaviness, distraction, and general negativity, or a spirit of joy? We don't think of being joyful as a responsibility, but that's exactly what it is.

It's all about perspective, isn't it? And perspective is a choice. What choice have you made this week? As a Christian, you are to be filled with joy because of who your God is and the hope your Father fills you with through the power of the Holy Spirit. The promises in His Word establish your secure future. That is why it's important to focus on what really matters: what God has said, what He has done, and what He has committed to do for you in eternity. That is exactly what Jesus did when He faced torture and death. Hebrews 12:1–2 says, "Since we are surrounded by so great a cloud of witnesses, let us lay aside every weight, and the sin which so easily ensnares us, and let us run with endurance the race that is set before us, looking unto Jesus, the author and finisher of our faith, who for the joy that was set before Him endured the cross, despising the shame, and has sat down at the right hand of the throne of God" (NKJV).

The joy that God is calling you to walk in is based not on circumstances but on the object of your faith and the future your Father ensures. Our Scripture this week speaks clearly of the power of where we place our faith and the importance of choosing to believe. The filling of joy and peace that God offers comes through *believing* (Rom. 15:13). It *is* a choice.

If you focus on the hope you have through faith in Christ, the goodness of the God you serve, and His promise to you of His presence now and of your eternal life in the future, your perspective will automatically change, regardless of today's pressures, challenges, or distractions, and you'll bring a spirit of joy into your home and marriage.

Reflection

- What kind of attitude have I been expressing at home this week?
- Am I taking the opportunity to be a joy-filled presence in our home by choosing faith, or is God asking me to change?
- What subjects should I avoid in order to protect my wife's joyful spirit?
- What truths can I share to help us both focus on being joyful in the Lord?

Application

This week, when you rise in the morning and first connect with your wife, greet her with a genuine smile, a positive spirit, and a positive comment.

Talk to her about one thing you're genuinely grateful to God for: for her as your wife, for God's provision, for His promises, for how He has blessed you recently, and so on. Speak words of faith and life into her heart.

Prayer

God my Father, You are calling me to walk in joy. I want to better reflect Your goodness to me in how I think and act in our home and around my wife. Please help me to remember the powerful role and responsibility I have in establishing the spirit of our home by my example and that joy is a choice You are calling me to make. This world is filled with darkness and challenges, but I don't need to let that weigh my spirit down. I see that what I think about and how I allow it to affect me is always a choice. Help me to clearly and consistently understand that my wife is responding to me and that I have a powerful impact on how she thinks and feels. Most of all, help me to choose joy based on who You are, what You have done for me, and the future You have promised. In Jesus's name, amen.

10

Like-Minded

Finally, all of you be of one mind, having compassion for one another; love as brothers, be tenderhearted, be courteous.

1 Peter 3:8 NKJV

As the spiritual rulers of the Jews observed Jesus's miracles and unmistakable spiritual authority, they correctly foresaw that unless something was done, their own power would be diminished. Men in power will do anything to keep it, as demonstrated by the Pharisees' preposterous claim that followed their observations of what Jesus had done: They accused Him of casting out demons by the power of Satan (Matt. 12:24). But Jesus made ashes of their ridiculous accusation by telling them that a house divided against itself cannot stand (v. 25).

It's true in a movement, business, governing party, or local church assembly, and it's certainly true in your marriage:

Dissension brings division. Division brings ineffectiveness and eventually dissolution.

Every instruction given to the church is universal, but let's remember that "the church" is the people—the body—and the application of this instruction, while spoken to the whole, is certainly and specifically directed to husband and wife: "Finally, *all of you*, have unity of mind" (1 Peter 3:8 ESV). If this truth isn't a reality in your marriage, it can never properly be lived out with the broader assembly of the church. It must first be true with you and your wife.

How will you lead your marriage relationship in this vital matter of being like-minded? As surely as Jesus Christ is the Cornerstone, a husband and wife's walking in unity is one of the foundation stones of His church at the local level. Your marriage is powerfully impacting the work of the church gathering you attend.

At first glance, it might seem that you are being instructed to make sure you and your wife agree on everything. But is this really what *like-minded* means in any biblical context? It can't be, because in any honest relationship, honest differences of opinion exist.

To be like-minded with your wife in the biblical sense is the same as being like-minded with other people in your local assembly: to be in fellowship with each other, pursuing peace together, being unified in spirit on the truths of central importance in God's Word. Make sure you are conforming to the truth of the gospel and the purpose of the church given in the Great Commission (Matt. 28:16–20). Therein lies why you are here and what you should be doing—it's what your marriage is for.

Many Christian husbands make being like-minded difficult for their wives. How can a wife be like-minded with her husband if he never speaks to her of what he believes or what he understands God's imperative to be for them? While you are the one commissioned to lead, governed by the Word, there may be times that being like-minded will require you to listen to your wife and change your wrong perspective.

If asked today, would your wife be able to articulate what the two of you are like-minded about regarding God, Jesus, the Spirit, the Word, and your purpose as a couple?

To be like-minded isn't an option but a direct instruction that can never come to reality in the church you attend if it isn't true in your marriage. The responsibility for being like-minded is shared, but your proactive leadership is required for being like-minded with your wife.

Reflection

- Are we like-minded (in fellowship and on the same page) when it comes to the major teachings of the Bible and the purpose of our marriage in the context of the Great Commission?
- How clear have I been in communicating these things?
- Does my wife feel that I am leading spiritually, or does she feel she is left to fend for herself?

Application

Understand that there can be no like-mindedness without walking with God. First John 1:7 says, "But if we walk in the light, as he is in the light, we have fellowship one with another, and the blood of Jesus Christ his Son cleanseth us from all sin" (KJV).

Take the time to learn and be able to communicate the gospel, the Great Commission, and the main doctrines of the Christian faith.

Discuss with your wife the subject of like-mindedness and the call of God on your marriage to walk in this biblical instruction.

Prayer

God my Father, when I consider how I've led my wife, it's obvious that I have some growing to do. But I want our marriage to be pleasing to You, and I see that You call us to be like-minded. I know that's a matter for the entire church, but it's clear to me that this is Your heart for us as a married couple. Lord, help us to let this instruction sink into our hearts, and help me to lead well by communicating to my wife Your desire for us to walk together in unity, the result of our walking individually with You. And help me to keep my eyes also on the big picture—the part that like-mindedness plays in the broader work of the church, the message You have given all of us to faithfully communicate to this dying world. Lord, I pray that You will find me faithful in all things. In Jesus's name, amen.

11

Delight

Behold, you are fair, my love!
Behold, you are fair!
You have dove's eyes.
    Song of Solomon 1:15 NKJV

There's nothing so natural as loving oneself. Outside of walking in the Spirit, it's the default approach for a man on any given day. So it's a bit surprising to discover in Ephesians 5—the chapter about marriage and selflessly laying down one's life—a strong encouragement for husbands to love themselves. "He who loves his wife loves himself" (v. 28 NKJV). This is a powerful, unexpected truth about one of the most effective ways a man can really love himself.

The love spoken of in this verse is agapē love—the selfless, unconditional kind of love. The Bible is teaching that husbands who love their wives selflessly and unconditionally are actually loving themselves in the same way.

Agapē also conveys the strong sense of being fond of her, loving her dearly, delighting in her. To what degree does your wife know that you think she is a truly wonderful person? Does she have the sense that you delight in her personality, her gifts, and her abilities?

Having strong feelings is never a substitute for communicating to her with your words. What a boost you give to her heart when she hears from you throughout the week about the various aspects of who she is that you truly delight in.

Why does the Word tell you that when you're doing these things, you're really loving yourself? First, the spiritual oneness that your marriage encompasses means that what is good for each part is good for the whole. When you build each other up, you're building up the entirety of your marriage.

There's also an aspect of human nature—how God made us all—that is manifested when you delight in your wife. Who doesn't enjoy a lighter spirit, a lift in their day, a more positive outlook when they know they are not only loved but genuinely liked by the people who know them the best?

The more you love your wife, the more you delight in who she is, the safer and freer her spirit will be to love you back. This is how a husband selflessly loves himself.

Reflection

- My wife knows I love her, but does she know I like her? That I delight in all the facets of who she is and enjoy spending time with her?
- When was the last time I communicated this aspect of my heart for her in a direct, verbal manner and then followed through with actions that prove my words to be true?
- What can I do this week to make sure she knows I take delight in her?

Application

- Three times this week, think of an aspect of your wife's character, personality, accomplishments, or way of being and take a moment to celebrate it with her.
- Tell your wife, "I think you're amazing when you [fill in the blank]" or, "I just love [fill in the blank] about you."
- Tell your wife you love spending time with her, and suggest a walk, drive, coffee date, or short getaway for the two of you.

Prayer

God my Father, it's easy to see how life keeps me from important things. You've told me that I'm loving myself when I'm loving my wife well. Help me to truly under-stand this principle in the context in which You gave it. I pray that this week my wife will have a stronger, renewed sense of how much I enjoy her as a person, how much I delight in her. Help me to communicate to her that I think she is a wonderful and truly amazing gift to me. In Jesus's name, amen.

12

Respect

Honor all people. Love the brotherhood. Fear God. Honor the king.

1 Peter 2:17 NKJV

The general admonition to honor all people—to value and treat everyone with respect—is not a difficult concept to understand. But how easy it is to pass over this instruction without a single thought of one's wife. Over the course of centuries, the Christian church has somehow made much of a wife's duty to respect her husband, while at the same time focusing little on a husband's equal duty to treat his wife with honor and respect.

A wife who is genuinely respected is a wife whose heart is open and ungrudging to the leadership of her husband. Conversely, a man who doesn't respect his wife is in the process of destroying his marriage. It really is that simple. There can be no true, wholesome oneness or love in a marriage without mutual respect. And it's not just a practical reality. It's a biblical imperative.

When a husband takes the time to consider his responsibility (and beautiful opportunity) to treat his wife with respect, suddenly every verbal and nonverbal interaction takes on the potential for immense positive power in the marriage. Mutual respect is at the very heart of unity in your home. And the power of this wisdom, missed by so many, can be deployed in a moment by your kind, respect-filled conversation and your consideration of your wife's thoughts, ideas, opinions, and needs.

Communicating respect to your wife is not difficult but neither does it happen without purpose and intention. It's natural to think of respecting others in terms of the ways and categories that cause you to feel respected. It's here where the careful consideration of your wife is needed. Have you taken the time to think about how she may be very different from you? In many cases, feeling respected is as straightforward as believing you have been genuinely heard and your perspective valued.

Yes, you need to have your wife's respect, but she has a deep need to be respected by you as well. If we are to hear the voice of the Holy Spirit in 1 Peter 2:17, the "Honor all people" inclusiveness of this teaching must begin with the closest relationship you have this side of heaven. It's not just about respecting all the people you may encounter "out there." It's about—especially about—the woman at your side, who has not only a deep need but the biblically sanctioned right to be honored and respected by you.

Reflection

Ask your wife these questions:

- Do you feel respected by me?
- Can you think of an experience in which I made you feel honored and respected?
- What can I do to contribute to your sense that I have deep respect for you?

Application

Establish your mindset: Cultivating respect in marriage is accomplished by seeking out your wife's thoughts, perspectives, and opinions instead of unilaterally making decisions that affect her and/or your family. A respected wife knows her husband genuinely cares about her perspective, her preferences, and her desires.

This week, purpose to seek her out on these matters and tell her, directly, that you have a deep, abiding respect for her.

Another way to make your wife feel respected is by following through, following up, and taking action after she has made a desire known or requested that something be done or changed.

Prayer

God my Father, I desire to grow and mature as a loving, godly husband. I know my wife has a need to be respected in our relationship. Please help me to understand my wife's heart so I can truly seek and value her perspective. Help me to have Your perspective on my wife—that she is Your gift to me and that You have uniquely equipped her to be a blessing in my life. This week, I purpose to walk in obedience with 1 Peter 2:17, starting in our home, with our marriage. I ask Your blessing on our marriage this week as I seek to communicate respect to my wife. In Jesus's name, amen.

13

Humility

And be clothed with humility, for

> "God resists the proud,
> But gives grace to the humble."
>
> 1 Peter 5:5 NKJV

You get dressed every morning, but do you dress in humility each day too? We're inclined to think of humility as a personality trait rather than an attitude to cultivate and a character trait to develop.

Left to ourselves, we avoid being humbled like rain clouds avoid the Mojave Desert. There is little in life more antithetical to the human spirit than humility, which can make sense in a world of growing belligerence. Choosing humility can seem unwise, unsafe, even dangerous. *If I humble myself, I'll be seen as weak. I'll get walked on or worse!*

And yet the Word instructs us to dress in humility every day. Clothes are to be put on. So, too, is humility. But what does it mean to be humble? If you're supposed to be leading your wife as her spiritual head, why are you being told to dress yourself with humility? Where's the leadership in that?

A humble husband isn't belligerent or passive-aggressive with his opinions and decisions. He doesn't focus on his own advantage, demand his rights, fight for what he's owed, or put himself forward, ensuring the bright lights are always trained on him. He knows his own capacity to make mistakes—to be wrong—which causes him to seek God's direction and approval and the wisdom and perspective of his wife.

Humility is the mindset and posture that has at its very core the settled conviction that God is truly and decisively in control. With that confident understanding and focus, what will happen next is not a concern. Humility says, "I'm in God's hands, and so are these circumstances."

Pride, on the other hand, deceives us into believing that we remain in control and must look after our own interests, regardless of the expense to others. Pride ensures that we are seen and heard and causes us to press our will on others.

Pride feels safe to our natural way of thinking but is a dangerous, destructive path because God has clearly indicated He is opposed to the proud. This is not some benign difference of opinion; He actively opposes those who choose to be prideful. And how foolish (dangerous) it is to place oneself directly in the crosshairs of God's opposition.

Pride and humility are ways of thinking, but they are equally and inescapably ways of being, which is to say pride and humility are relational. They always manifest themselves in relation to things and other people—your wife, for instance.

Does pride make regular appearances—large or small—in your marriage? The spiritual character of a man walking in the Spirit is humility—it's an internal posture that inescapably manifests itself in your life.

When it comes to living with your wife, pride, like anger, destroys what it touches—you, your marriage, your testimony. And when it comes to the pride that is so natural to the flesh, you have two options: humble yourself or be humbled.

God states clearly that He hates pride.

> The fear of the Lord is to hate evil;
> Pride, arrogance, the evil way,
> And the perverted mouth, I hate. (Prov. 8:13 NASB)

Pride invites the opposition of God as surely and effectively as it closes the heart of your wife. The good news is pride or humility is always a choice. Are you known by your wife and others to be a humble man? What choice are you making this week?

Reflection

- Ask yourself: Am I a prideful person?
- Ask your wife: Do you often find me prideful in our interactions and in my responses to you?

If you and your wife are often at odds with each other throughout the week, pride is at the root of it! The Bible tells us contention comes from pride (Prov. 13:10).

Application

Listen to the Spirit's prompting. The next time you are interacting with your wife and you feel the intensity in yourself rising, stop. Just stop! Recognize that what is taking place in you in that moment is a spiritual battle.

Lower the intensity. Genuinely listen. Speak respectfully and calmly and, by the power of the Spirit that indwells you, choose humility.

Remember, it's impossible to have an argument with a humble person.

Prayer

God my Father, You have made it clear in Your Word that humility is not an option but that You require humility of every person. It's equally clear how important humility is in a close, loving marriage. The only wise path is to walk before You in the spirit of humility, yet my own will is so quick to rise up in pride. Lord, please do Your refining work in my heart. May I grow and mature as a husband who chooses to be humble in all my interactions with my wife so that our home will be a place where Your Spirit reigns. In Jesus's name, amen.

14

Friendship

A man who has friends must himself be friendly,
But there is a friend who sticks closer than a
brother.

Proverbs 18:24 NKJV

Friendship—it was your wife's dream before you married and, if the choices of life haven't closed hearts and opened exits, it's still her dream today. She continues to desire a close friendship with you. Are you your wife's friend?

One sure piece of evidence that a marriage is on solid biblical ground is when a husband has found the best of friends in his wife. Deep friendship is the natural, normal state of a godly marriage, where every vulnerability and weakness is safe, every strength is celebrated, and trust is uncompromised. Have you and your wife found this level of deep, spiritual friendship?

Friendship requires two, but it must start with you. You have the commission from God to love your wife as Jesus loves His bride, the church. The mere fact of being married is never adequate to meet the needs of your wife's heart. And it certainly doesn't guarantee friendship in your relationship. Deep friendship in any relationship doesn't just happen. This reality is as true in marriage as it is anywhere else. If there is to be a growing friendship between you and your wife, it will have to be built.

The marriage with little or no friendship may make it for a while, even a long season. But your wife's needs can never be fully met without friendship on your life's journey together.

She knows instinctively that your marriage was intended by God to yield more than a functional business partnership. For every couple, an unanticipated place in the future awaits where the fact that you got married is not enough for the need of the moment—the need to nurture and protect the secret place in your wife's heart, which is where the hope of your oneness lives. And what you do then will depend on what you did to prepare your marriage for life's mountaintops and valleys.

God designed the two of you to be more than just married. He designed you to be lovers who are great friends, but friendship only grows where it is cultivated. True friendship in marriage isn't about a fact—a marriage certificate. Friendship is the fruit of loving unity that has been cultivated over time. She desired to be your friend when you got married. She still desires friendship with you on the deepest level as the years pass.

The Scripture above speaks of the importance of being friendly if friends are to be had. In obedience to the wisdom of God's Word, and in blessing your wife, seek to cultivate friendship with her this week as the normal pursuit of the marriage God intends for you.

Reflection

- Ask yourself: Am I friendly toward my wife?
- Ask your wife:
  - I'm your husband, but am I a good friend to you?
  - What could I do to build a stronger friendship with you?
  - When you think of our friendship, what are the top three things that come to mind?

Application

Being a good friend requires considering what the other person values, appreciates, and needs from you. For example, my wife, Lisa, is an introvert. She needs downtime. Friendship with her includes my ensuring she isn't booked back-to-back all week because I said yes to every opportunity.

Remember, friendship requires cultivation, conversation, consideration . . . and time together.

Set aside some time this week to think about tangible ways you can make friendship with your wife a priority.

Prayer

God my Father, I desire to be a close, deep friend to my wife as we live our married lives together. Give me discernment to understand her well and a ready mind to show her my care for her needs. And help me to truly listen to her heart this week as she shares her thoughts and concerns with me. May our closeness and friendship grow deep as we cultivate it in our marriage. In Jesus's name, amen.

15

Peace

You will keep him in perfect peace,
Whose mind is stayed on You,
Because he trusts in You.

Isaiah 26:3 NKJV

If there's one thing this world is adept at destroying, it would have to be inner peace. Regardless of the vast increase in knowledge, inventions to make life better, and unprecedented increases in wealth, for many people peace remains elusive much, if not most, of the time. Based on how you lead, will your home be a place of peace this week? Was it a peaceful place last week?

The often-missed truth about peace is that it has nothing to do with "place." A close friend of mine manages the portfolios of multibillionaires. Though nothing is denied them, peace eludes almost every one of them. Peace (or its absence) is the state of one's heart, not the state of one's circumstances.

The home you lead each week can never be a peaceful place unless you bring to it a spirit of peace. And your wife will never be at peace unless you are at peace. That's the price that oneness cannot avoid paying. As a husband, you have a responsibility to seek and then walk in peace. It's part of your leadership role in establishing the godly culture of your home.

Where will you find the peace in your soul that evades so many? The Bible brings a clear, easily understood answer that is so direct, so succinctly stated, that it's easily missed. As it is for most men, the list of things that disturb your peace may be long. But in response to every item on that list, God says that to find and maintain inner peace, there is something you must do: You must keep your mind focused and fixed on Him because you trust in Him.

No circumstance, however catastrophic, is a match for God's peace pursued God's way. And that's the real challenge, isn't it—pursuing peace God's way? Sometimes we're like Naaman of 2 Kings 5, who desired to be healed but felt believing and simply obeying weren't enough. Does this describe you at times? Wanting something more difficult to do than merely unyieldingly, steadfastly believing?

To bring peace into your home is to entrust your circumstances and all the peace-destroying messes of this life to God. Do you trust God? Is your mind fixed on Him for the challenges to inner peace that this week holds for you?

Reflection

- Have I been walking in peace, or have I been exuding a spirit of unrest and a lack of faith in God's provision and sovereignty?
- How has the spirit of peace or turmoil that I regularly bring into our home impacted my wife?

Application

Put your circumstances in their place. They may be uncomfortable, they may be hard, but God is present with you and is over all. Tell yourself at night when you go to bed and in the morning when you rise that God is in control. Life doesn't surprise Him or catch Him off guard.

State out loud, "My trust is in God. Today I put my trust in Him."

Remember that to have your mind "stayed on God" you must discipline your mind to keep your thoughts on Him throughout the day and remain confident in His will for you.

Prayer

God my Father, thank You for Your promise to keep me in perfect peace when I keep my mind focused on You. I desire to have the kind of focus and trust in You that keeps inner turmoil far from me, my wife, and our home. I see in Your Word the responsibility I have to act—to

discipline my mind. I also recognize in myself the incli-
nation to let challenges and bad circumstances become
my focus, robbing me of the peace You give. Lord, how I
need Your presence every moment in my life. Help me to
listen to Your voice this week as I draw near to You and
keep my focus on You. Thank You, my Lord and my God.
In Jesus's name, amen.

16

Asking Forgiveness

Confess your faults one to another, and pray one for another, that ye may be healed. The effectual fervent prayer of a righteous man availeth much.

James 5:16 KJV

The Bible doesn't say, "If you're caught red-handed in sin, then you should confess." It says confess now. Be proactive. James 5:16 is one of those Bible verses that is far easier to agree with in theory than to follow through with in practice.

There's a reason confession is never our first choice. We naturally hate being in a position of weakness, and this is the message of your Enemy: Confessing makes you a weak, pitiful man. But Jesus didn't come to torment your flesh. He came to kill it. Confession is difficult because it always involves a funeral. This is why we recoil from talking about our sin. We don't like death, especially ours.

For most husbands, it's humbling and difficult to merely mouth the words "I'm sorry" to your wife after you've done something hurtful, selfish, thoughtless, stupid, and sinful. But what about the sins you've kept hidden from her? Talking about those is like torture before the funeral. Jesus knows something about torture, yet He still said to take up your cross daily (Luke 9:23).

Before we confess our sins quickly and move on with the speed of someone vacating a burning building, we need to know what confession actually involves. Merely admitting—saying—what you've done is not confession or a true seeking of forgiveness. Judas did that.

The kind of confession that is meaningful to God is genuine brokenness—being truly sorry for what you have done, turning away from the sin, and seeking His mercy. "The sacrifices of God are a broken spirit: a broken and a contrite heart, O God, thou wilt not despise" (Ps. 51:17 KJV).

When you've come face-to-face with the reality of what you've done and the damage caused, the only appropriate response is confession. Seeking forgiveness includes honestly, openly stating what you've done and owning the reality of it—being broken—and humbly asking to be forgiven.

To choose confession and seek forgiveness is always God's path for the Christian and is essential to Spirit-led leadership in your home.

Reflection

- Have I done anything unloving this week for which I need forgiveness from my wife?
- Have I kept secret sins from her, telling myself it would only hurt her if I confessed?
- Am I humble, quick to acknowledge my wrongdoing and to ask for forgiveness?

Application

If you committed a quick offense in the moment, deal with it quickly. Immediately acknowledge your sin, communicate true sorrow for what you did and how it hurt her, and then humbly ask her to forgive you. If she doesn't forgive you right away, that's okay. Choose not to take offense. Rather, choose to be loving and holy toward her, allowing God to do His work in her heart.

If you hid something from her, first get on your knees before God and repent (turn from the sin) and ask His forgiveness. Then select a quiet moment and place where you won't be interrupted. Humbly (many have wisely gotten on their knees) tell her what you did. Communicate true brokenness for the damage, pain, betrayal, and heartache you brought into your marriage. Own these things without using a single qualifier, excuse, or accusation against her. Then ask her to forgive you. She may well need time to process what happened. Give her that time. In the meantime, ask for God's mercy, help, and protection for your marriage.

Depending on the nature of your offense, you may need to involve godly, wise, unbiased, biblical mentors to be with the two of you in the process.

You are one before the Lord. Therefore, there can be no secrets between you.

Prayer

God my Father, Your Word makes it clear we all need forgiveness. Your Word says You oppose the proud but give grace to the humble. Lord, I need Your mercy and grace. I desire to be a humble husband. Please help me to readily check my will and my pride and to be quick to repent to my wife when I sin against her. Please help my wife to forgive me. And may I grow to maturity in my walk with You so those moments when I cause pain in her heart are absent from our marriage. In Jesus's name, amen.

17

Granting Forgiveness

Bearing with one another, and forgiving each other, whoever has a complaint against anyone; just as the Lord forgave you, so must you do also.

Colossians 3:13 NASB

Someone once said that the best marriages are made up of two good forgivers. There's wisdom in that statement because as great as the Creator intended it to be, married life is filled with opportunities to be a good forgiver.

Where forgiveness is practiced, humility, redemption, and love flourish. Where forgiveness isn't practiced, resentment and bitterness grow. And like a tiny root under a building, bitterness left unchecked by true forgiveness grows until the foundation is destroyed.

There's a reason people rub their hands together on a cold day. Friction produces heat. Which is great in the right context, but the proximity in marriage inevitably produces friction and heat of another kind from time to time. Who you truly are reveals itself in the everyday crucible of your principal human relationship.

And it's here in the closeness of marriage where granting forgiveness is most needed if oneness is to be maintained and God's purposes in your marriage are to be realized.

The irony and seeming unfairness of forgiveness is that it's always the offended person, the person who has been on the receiving end of someone else's sin, who is called on to forgive. To the natural mind, it's backward. The offender is the person who should pay. Have you felt this at times? Have you ever wanted your wife to pay before you forgive?

That's not the approach God took with us, is it? Romans 5:8 says, "But God commendeth [proves] his love toward us, in that, while we were yet sinners, Christ died for us" (KJV). He offered His forgiveness before we even recognized the depth of our need for it.

The forgiveness heaven offered you—and you are required to offer your wife—is a costly gift that, if it is to be truly given, requires you to sacrifice two things: (1) the moral high ground and (2) the pain that was caused. And when the pain of the offense cuts to the bone, that can seem extremely unfair. But it is God's way.

True forgiveness removes any thought of the moral high ground between you and your wife. When the prodigal's father met his returning son—who had squandered everything, brought shame to the family name, and lived like the devil—he raised his son from his penitent position to his feet, embraced him, and brought him into open fellowship. There is no continuing condemnation in the Father's forgiveness. There should be none in yours either, and if your flesh is sacrificed on the altar of God's grace when you forgive, there won't be.

The pain caused by the sin or offense also must be sacrificed. God knows exactly what to do with your pain, anger, embarrassment, or frustration. He'll receive it, but He won't take it from you. You must give it to Him. If you are hanging on to the pain, you haven't truly forgiven.

Forgiving and offering mercy require humility. The easiest approach in the moment is to ignore everything until the bad vibes blow over. Yet you and your wife will only move forward in fellowship and oneness if you are willing to forgive.

Reflection

- Yes, God has forgiven me, but do I forgive my wife the same way? Am I a ready forgiver or a begrudging forgiver?
- Do I keep a record of past (supposedly forgiven) offenses?
- Has my leadership in our marriage been marked by forgiveness, or am I inclined to avoid offenses?
- Is there a way in which God is asking me to change?

Application

In a neutral moment (not after an offense or when emotions are high), purpose to set aside time to discuss forgiveness in your marriage.

Don't come with expectations of what your wife needs to do, but only discuss what God is asking you to do. Discuss God's requirement for forgiveness.

Be humble and bold to ask if there is anything you need to seek forgiveness for, and guard against defensiveness regarding offenses that may be brought up.

Prayer

God my Father, You have forgiven so much. You have loved me despite my failures, and the truth is I need Your forgiveness regularly. I pray that I would show to my wife the same loving graciousness You have shown to me. Lord, please bring healing where it is needed as we offer the grace to each other that You have so freely given each of us. In Jesus's name, amen.

18

Anxiety

Do not be anxious about anything, but in everything by prayer and supplication with thanksgiving let your requests be made known to God.

Philippians 4:6 ESV

Our current century seems tailor-made to create anxiety in our souls. From personal tensions to global chaos, there is much to be anxious about. Anxiety is a logical response to the crazy uncertainty of these times in which we live.

But Paul was writing in the first—not the twenty-first—century, with Christians heading toward approximately 140 years of persecution. As it turns out, there are enough anxiety-inducing experiences to span the centuries.

In the midst of it all, as if the Holy Spirit doesn't really know your situation, you're told simply, "Don't do it . . . don't be anxious about anything." Maybe you don't call it "anxiety" or "being anxious" when referring to yourself. You may use other words, like *apprehension, worry, angst, uncertainty* . . . but they all add up to the same thing: being anxious. And the Bible instructs us never to go there.

In marriage, your anxiety is like a virus, naturally spreading to your wife's heart. You wouldn't choose it for her; it just happens. And she'll absorb your unsettled spirit like a dry sponge in a puddle. Anxiety destroys the peace in your home even though it is completely impotent to bring about any positive change or desired result.

By following the Bible's instruction not to be anxious, you are protecting more than your heart and state of mind. You're protecting your wife's heart and inner peace too. God's way of oneness in marriage makes you a channel of His peace in your home. But how are you to "not be anxious"?

From a biblical perspective, it's straightforward: prayer, supplication, thanksgiving, directly appealing to God for the specific request you have on your mind.

You know what prayer is: communication with God. But in Philippians 4:6, you're told to pray in a specific way. Yes, you're told to make your request to God about the item troubling you. You're even told to ask God earnestly (supplicate) about the matter, but none of your ardent seeking of God is to happen apart from thankfulness.

When you're troubled, anxious about something, God says in effect, "Approach Me about the matter, but approach with a thankful heart." It is here that God makes the most amazing promise: After you've done as He instructs, He promises to give you a peace that passes understanding—that makes no sense, given the circumstances. It's supernatural—a peace that can't be explained apart from Him. It's His gift to you, available according to His instructions.

With every instruction He gives, God also includes the means and the power to follow through. Say no to anxiety God's way, protecting the spirit of your home, along with your wife's heart and your own.

Reflection

According to the Word, anxiety is unnecessary and can be directly dealt with.

- Ask yourself:
  - □ Have I been treating anxiety in my life as the enemy it is?
  - □ Have I been walking in anxiety and treating it like it's a normal part of Christian life?
- Ask your wife: How are you affected when I communicate anxiety about something I'm facing?

Application

Anxiety is the same as a malicious intruder in your home. When you feel those first icy shards of anxiety in your heart, recognize this as an attack from the Enemy and take action immediately.

- Make a list of everything you are thankful to God for.
- Bow before God and begin praising Him for all the things you are genuinely thankful for.

- Bring your specific request about the situation to God. Tell Him what it is that you desire to happen. It's God's burden now. Leave it with Him and receive His peace.
- Find a time to come together with your wife to discuss the topic and the solution God offers in Philippians 4:6.

Prayer

God my Father, I don't usually see anxiety as an attack from Your Enemy and mine, but I want to change that—to have Your mind on this matter. Please help me respond immediately and turn to You in thankfulness and praise when the Enemy strikes. And Lord, help me to do what You say—to bring my requests to You, knowing that You hear me and remembering that You are all-powerful, that nothing is out of Your oversight. You are asking me to have faith, to trust You, and, consequently, to demonstrate to my wife the path of peace. May I guard her heart with Your truth. In Jesus's name, amen.

19

Service

But by love serve one another.

Galatians 5:13 KJV

We tend to think of loving others by serving as doing the things we choose to do for them.

That's exactly what Cain told himself he was doing when he brought his sacrifice to God. Of course, Cain brought his best. After all, it was from him and for God. It needed to be the best. How do we know this was Cain's posture? If he had brought a lesser sacrifice that he believed was unworthy, he wouldn't have reacted as he did when God refused it: furious that his sacrifice—his service to God—was rejected (Gen. 4:3–5).

And why was his sacrifice shunned? Because, under the guise of loving God, Cain was actually loving himself by offering service to God on his own terms. Those who love God serve on His terms, not their own.

Many people "serving" in church are serving in the same spirit as Cain rather than in the Spirit of Christ. They have a particular gift from the Holy Spirit for use in the church, but they ignore the Word's instructions about how to govern that gift to be edifying, according to the Spirit who gave it in the first place. They ignore how God has said they should serve Him. Like Cain, they're serving on their own terms, not God's.

Serving in marriage is no different. It's natural and common for spouses to serve on their own terms rather than on the priorities, desires, and needs of the other person.

Are you quick to serve your wife *if* it suits your schedule? Are you willing to serve her, provided you choose what that service will look like, when it will happen, where it will take place, and for how long, regardless of your wife's heart, desires, and true needs? That is service on your own terms. Is that the spirit of true, godly serving of one another? Is that serving your spouse in a manner that says "I love you" rather than communicates "I love me"?

Service on our own terms may feel like we're offering a genuine gift from the heart. That's certainly what we tell ourselves. But service on these terms is only serving oneself as Cain did, on his terms rather than on God's.

When you choose to serve another—your wife—on her terms rather than yours, you are truly serving as unto the Lord, not giving out of convenience to yourself . . . not giving to get but giving to love. And that service is service unto God as He desires of you and as He requires of you. When self is removed from service, the love of Christ is being shared.

On whose terms will you serve your wife this week?

Reflection

- Do I have a servant's heart?
- Do I truly love to serve my wife in ways that say "I love you" to her?
- Has the spirit of Cain crept into my heart when it comes to serving my wife?
- Do I truly serve out of selfless love, or am I serving on my own terms?

Application

Look for opportunities to serve your wife this week. Don't keep score. Let God do that. If you do, you're serving to get, not serving to love.

Ask your wife to name a few ways you could serve her better. If you're already great at this, God bless you. Keep (humbly) providing a selfless example!

Prayer

God my Father, thank You for my wife. May I always remind myself that she is Your gift to me. May I see her as You see her—beautiful and precious. Lord, You've told me to serve her in love. Help me to see the many opportunities that present themselves each day. I pray that she will experience from me this week service that comes from selflessly loving her in ways that are meaningful to her. In Jesus's name, amen.

20

Desire

I am my beloved's, and his desire is toward me.

Song of Solomon 7:10 KJV

A new husband doesn't have to be told to desire his wife. Nothing comes more naturally. And yet the Lord still felt it necessary to remind that same husband to continue to desire his wife through the years:

> Let your fountain be blessed,
>   and rejoice in the wife of your youth,
>   a lovely deer, a graceful doe.
> Let her breasts fill you *at all times* with delight;
>   *be intoxicated always* in her love. (Prov. 5:18–19 ESV)

When it comes to sexuality and passion, the world has nothing, literally nothing, to teach the biblical Christian. The Bible begins with two naked people in a pristine garden, gives instruction on living passionately and faithfully together, and includes one of the most romantic, steamy, beautiful depictions of a husband and wife living as God intended in the Song of Solomon.

God teaches what you need to know and what to make habitual in your marriage. After a few (maybe many) years of marriage, are you still choosing to desire your wife?

God gives you His admonition to desire your wife because sin destroyed the garden of Eden and will seek to tear down everything in your marriage that is right, good, true, and beautiful.

Without purpose and vigilance, desire for one's wife will atrophy like a muscle that is no longer used. In a Christian marriage, this doesn't usually happen because a man decides engaging with his wife is no longer important; it typically happens because the natural course of life buries this priority with a thousand other important or urgent needs, giving the Enemy an opportunity to dish up counterfeits in unsuspecting moments.

There is no place for passive husbands in a biblical marriage. All the instruction in the Word to you regarding your wife is about pursuing her, loving her, and caring for her, just as Jesus pursues His bride.

What does it mean to truly desire your wife? The Scriptures above speak of pursuing your wife sexually, but there's more to the instruction than sex. When the Bible says, "Let your fountain be blessed" and "let her breasts satisfy you," these are more than casual references. God is calling on you to take action—to purpose in your heart and in your physical expression to make sure these things happen.

God places the responsibility for this pursuit directly on you—the husband. Desiring your wife isn't always something that happens by itself, especially as the complications of life build over the years. This is why you are told to engage, to pursue desiring your wife.

Where your priorities are established, your action is sure to follow. Embrace the Bible's instruction to desire your wife and ensure that there is no counterfeit weaving its way into your heart and mind.

Does your wife know you desire her? Does she know she is the only source of sexual pleasure you will allow into your heart, mind, and body? Many men wonder why their wives don't enjoy sex with them, and for many it's because the husband doesn't pursue and desire her in the fullness of who she is and what she gives. Give to your wife your genuine, single-minded love, desiring her as God instructed you to do "at all times" (Prov. 5:19 KJV).

Is your wife's heart waiting today to be filled with the confidence that comes from a husband who truly desires her?

God has given the instruction. Take action.

Reflection

- Have I fallen into a rut, taking my wife for granted and not communicating my desire for her?
- When was the last time I expressed through my words, countenance, and actions that I desire my wife and no other?
- Do I know meaningful ways to communicate this to her?

Application

Don't neglect pursuing your wife sexually. Tell your wife directly, "My love [or 'babe,' or insert your own endearment], your breasts satisfy me . . . you satisfy me. I will never allow my heart or mind to wander from the sexual pleasure I have in you."

Tell her how pleased you are with her, and if you've forgotten or never known meaningful ways to communicate your desire for her, ask her what says, "I desire you."

Prayer

God my Father, You have blessed me with the most amazing gift in my wife. Thank You for all the fun we enjoy together in the day—and when the lights go out! You are the good Father who knows how to give good gifts, and I'm so grateful to You for her. Lord, remind me—prompt me by Your Spirit—to regularly communicate to her that she is ever, only and always, the source of my desire and sensual pleasure. Lord, may You and she find me faithful in these things. In Jesus's name, amen.

21

Patience

With all lowliness and meekness, with longsuffering, forbearing one another in love.

Ephesians 4:2 KJV

Reading through the Old Testament, one quickly sees how patient God was with the children of Israel. Maybe you've read an account of God's dealings with them and found yourself shaking your head. *How could they so quickly turn away from God after all He did for them?* Of course, you would never be so easily led away from God, right? Every man who has read the first five books of the Bible has had similar thoughts.

But then you recall your personal walk with God, and you're faced with the reality of how many times you didn't have faith. How many times you've turned your back on the Father and pursued your own agenda, interests, and lusts . . . and yet, as the good Father that He is, He waited for you to return to Him. How loving, how patient, has the Father been with you?

God was incredibly patient with the children of Israel. God has been equally patient with you—too many times to count. Which invites a question: Do you extend to your wife the same grace you have repeatedly received? Are you patient with her? Do you master your responses and respond with a voice and body language that isn't clipped, sharp, sarcastic, or generally impatient? What is your wife's experience when you want something immediately or when you expected a situation to turn out differently than it did? Does she think, "I sure appreciate my husband. He's so patient with me"?

We've often heard it said that patience is a virtue—a mark of good character. And it is, but the Bible says patience is far more than just a virtue. Patience is the evidence of the Holy Spirit's presence in your life. "The fruit of the Spirit is . . . patience" (Gal. 5:22 ESV). A man who is filled with the Spirit is a patient man.

But the biblical definition doesn't end there. The Bible declares that patience is also the manifestation of loving another person. Maybe you've never made the connection between being patient and loving your wife, but the Bible is very clear. First Corinthians 13:4 says, "Love is patient" (ESV).

How loving does your wife find you to be by this biblical standard? How filled with the Spirit and loving will she find you this week?

Reflection

- Am I consistently patient with my wife in the face of stress, problems, and circumstances that turn out differently than I wanted them to?
- Would my wife tell me I am a patient man?
- What circumstance or situation keeps coming up to which I can change my response and choose to be patient (loving) instead of impatient?
- Do I need to confess to my wife and ask her forgiveness?

Application

- Name it and own it: Impatience is sinful, self-focused behavior.
- Think through this past week: When were you impatient?
- Believe that you are not a victim of your personality or your flesh. Impatience (or patience) is a choice you make every time.
- Purpose to be in communion with God and to walk in the Spirit today and this week.

Prayer

God my Father, I confess to You that I've not been as patient—as loving—as I should have been with my wife. I want to see this fruit of the Spirit increase in me. Please help me to see my next temptation to be impatient with her as an opportunity to respond the way You desire me to respond. I pray that both You and she will see a genuine change in me this week as I stop using the excuses I've used in the past to be impatient and instead choose loving self-control. In Jesus's name, amen.

22

Tenderhearted

And be ye kind one to another, tenderhearted, forgiving one another, even as God for Christ's sake hath forgiven you.

Ephesians 4:32 KJV

It's easy to say we agree with the general admonitions of Scripture. And here again we encounter the phrase "one to another"—that broad category involving the whole church. Be tenderhearted—it's the right way to treat each other in the church. Yet, in a strange twist of irony, it's easy to forget to be consistently tenderhearted within the closeness of the marriage relationship. It's common to bypass one's wife when considering admonitions that apply to everyone.

Although the instruction in Ephesians is universal, the application is personal, down to the people you encounter and interact with each day, starting with your wife. Are you a tenderhearted man when interacting with her, day in and day out?

What exactly does it mean to be tenderhearted? An old French proverb popularized in English in the 1700s says, "God tempers the wind to the shorn lamb." These few words are a metaphor for someone facing the challenges of life in a vulnerable, weakened state. The loving Father takes note of the condition of that particular lamb (person) and regulates the wind (adversity) being faced, making the lamb safe from the worst of the elements. Here are some verses that show God's tender heart toward us:

- "The Lord is near to the brokenhearted and saves the crushed in spirit" (Ps. 34:18 ESV).
- "He heals the brokenhearted and binds up their wounds" (Ps. 147:3 ESV).
- "A bruised reed he will not break, and a faintly burning wick he will not quench" (Isa. 42:3 ESV).
- "Because of the tender mercy of our God, whereby the sunrise shall visit us from on high to give light to those who sit in darkness and in the shadow of death, to guide our feet into the way of peace" (Luke 1:78–79 ESV).
- "And he arose and came to his father. But while he was still a long way off, his father saw him and felt compassion, and ran and embraced him and kissed him" (Luke 15:20 ESV).

When we have eyes to see, the goodness of our Father's heart comes into clear view. He is loving, gracious, and tenderhearted toward us. And when we have ears to hear, we come to understand that this is the call of God on our life . . . on the life of a husband.

To be tenderhearted toward your wife is far more than warm, kind feelings about her. The tenderhearted husband thinks about who his wife is as a unique person and considers where she is emotionally and spiritually. He contemplates where she might be feeling weak and vulnerable and when she may be feeling physically or emotionally fragile.

The tenderhearted husband verbally communicates to his wife that he cares deeply for how she is doing, and he understands that she needs to hear gentle, tender words that convince her she is loved, considered, and cared for.

God is a God of action. In His love and care for His people, the Father tempers (softens, diminishes) the wind to the shorn lamb. The tenderhearted husband is a man of action too. His care for his wife moves him to change what he can to better meet the needs of the shorn lamb he is caring for.

When tenderheartedness is in action, there is no accounting for the cost, time, effort, or trouble it takes to love in this way. It is an honor to be entrusted by God with the heart of His gift to you, your wife. Serving your wife with a tender heart is loving her according to the example of your Father. For tenderheartedness to be an authentic reality in the church, it must first be true in your marriage.

Reflection

- Have I made being tenderhearted toward my wife the priority that God has made it for everyone in His church?
- Does my wife have the sense that she is safe, that I will care for her in her times of weakness and need?
- Do my words and tone consistently reflect a tender-hearted spirit in our marriage?

Application

Embrace the admonition to be tenderhearted as God's instruction for you, starting with your marriage. By the power of the Holy Spirit, this is who God is calling you to be.

Tenderheartedness in action in your marriage is caring for your wife in meaningful ways. This begins with regular assessments of her: Where is she emotionally, physically, spiritually? Be on the lookout for those times when she will need you to express your tenderness toward her.

Regulate the way you speak to her this week to ensure that your tone communicates care and love.

Prayer

God my Father, I see clearly that You desire this fruit of the Spirit in my life, especially as it relates to my wife and our marriage. I ask You to prompt me by Your Spirit whenever I begin to stray from the path of communicating with tenderheartedness toward my wife. May she experience this week the love of Christ in me and truly have a sense of being considered and cared for so that together we can better represent who You are, as well as Your love for the world. In Jesus's name, amen.

23

Sacrifice

Greater love hath no man than this, that a man lay down his
life for his friends.

John 15:13 KJV

He was the King. Every king must have a crown. The crown
selected was met with approval and cheers by everyone
present. Deemed appropriate for the coronation, it was sized
accurately and fit securely on His head. Even though the celebration that followed involved much rigorous physical activity,
the crown would remain in place. Long, hardened, unyielding
thorns with tips sharper than ice picks ensured it would remain
secure. Once shoved down, deep into the scalp of that noble
head, it would not be moved.

Hours before, wrestling in anguish at the prospect of what
His body was about to endure—the horror, the pain, and being

forsaken by the Father—Jesus's soul was brought to a place of overwhelming agony. His body responded to the mental strain and began sweating profusely until He was drenched and huge drops dripped off His head.

Isaiah 52:14 describes the outcome of the crucifixion like this: "His appearance was so disfigured that he did not look like a man, and his form did not resemble a human being" (csb).

Jesus was scourged with the Roman flagrum, or flagellum—a method of punishment specifically designed to cut, lacerate, and pick the flesh off of bones with each blow, resulting in torture so extreme that, in the end, the victim doesn't even look like a human being, just as Isaiah said.

Eusebius, writing in the fourth century, described the results of Roman scourging on the body:

> The sufferer's veins were laid bare and the very muscles and tendons and bowels of the victim were open to exposure.

Is it any wonder that Jesus, fully apprised of what awaited Him, asked the Father to "let this cup pass from me" (Matt. 26:39 kjv)?

Jesus took the punishment for the sins of humankind. He sacrificed Himself for you—for His bride, the church. Real sacrifice is to lay down one's life as Jesus did. Real sacrifice is the essence of love, the love you have received instead of the condemnation and judgment you deserve.

What, exactly, are you willing to sacrifice today for your wife?

Do you have the mind of Christ? Do you lead a life of willing, true, loving sacrifice for your wife? Are you laying down your life? This is what you are told to do in the Word—to love her as Jesus loves the church "*and gave himself for it*" (Eph. 5:25 kjv).

The call of God is on you—on your life—to sacrifice yourself . . . not to be willing to sacrifice but to actually do it, to actually die to yourself, to give all for your wife, just as Jesus gave all for you.

This sacrifice of love has no thought of give and take with your wife, an agreement where the 50/50 principle is fairly applied. Search as you will, nowhere in the Word is your wife told to sacrifice in this way for you. The willing (not begrudging) sacrifice of laying down one's life in marriage is for you alone. Are you willing to give like that? To love like that? Are you willing to give yourself for your wife like Jesus Christ gave Himself for His bride?

And why are you called to do this? Because your marriage is not what you are doing with your life; your marriage is what God is doing in the world, for His glory. Your marriage shows others how deeply Jesus Christ loves the church.

Are you ready to live a life of obedience, a life of true sacrifice for the wife God blessed you with for His purposes in the world?

Reflection

- Do I look at my role as husband as requiring that I lay down my life for my wife?
- Is there anything in my life that says while I love my wife, I don't really have to sacrifice for her?

Application

Recognize that true sacrifice never comes without a price to the one sacrificing, and real sacrifice is always given ungrudgingly, without a guaranteed return.

Remember that Jesus sacrificed His life in the flesh and so must you. Look for opportunities in your week, month, and year to lay down your life—your natural desires, your plans— for your wife.

The sacrificial love of Jesus is a present reality, not a one-time event. The sacrificial life doesn't rest on past moments of sacrifice but is lived out in the present.

Prayer

God my Father, how unnatural it is for me to want to sacrifice myself—my hopes, dreams, plans, and desires— for another. I'd much rather help when it doesn't cost me anything, but I know You are calling me to embrace the Word, to take into my heart the gift of loving sacrifice I have received, and to be a true disciple of Jesus Christ, laying down my life for the wife You have given me to love the way Jesus loves His bride, the church. Oh God, help me to put down my rebel flesh. I know I can do this only by walking in fellowship with You, by the power of the Holy Spirit, and I pray that my wife will see Christ in me this week. I pray that she will experience the sacrificial love You have called me to walk in. In Jesus's name, amen.

24

Contentment

I have learned to be content in whatever circumstances I find myself.

Philippians 4:11 CSB

Those who have chosen to be content have removed a powerful weapon from the Enemy's arsenal. This is one of the reasons Paul tells Timothy in 1 Timothy 6:6 that "godliness with contentment is great gain" (KJV). Where contentment reigns, strivings cease.

Discontent is a powerful motivator for ungodliness in the life of the believer. Has the spirit of discontent ever wrapped its deceitful tentacles around your mind and heart?

At times, the Enemy doesn't need any help; a Christian man can walk the road to discontent all on his own. At other times, the temptation to be discontent comes directly from the Enemy, as we see from the very beginning with Eve in the garden of Eden (Gen. 3 NKJV).

This is the approach of the Enemy:

- To call into question what God has clearly stated: "Has God indeed said, 'You shall not eat of every tree of the garden?'" (v. 1). It's just an innocent question, right? Of course, he knows the answer, but he wants to draw Eve into conversation.
- To cast doubt on and twist the words of God: "You will not surely die" (v. 4). This is the very reason Satan doesn't want you to know the Word. If you don't read and know what the Bible says, how will you be able to spot a counterfeit message?
- To slander the goodness of God and cast aspersions on His intentions. "God knows that in the day you eat of it your eyes will be opened, and you will be like God, knowing good and evil" (v. 5).
- To get you to engage with him, to give him a moment for a harmless conversation, so he can press his agenda. But whether the discontent comes from your desires or the devil, you are responsible for dealing with it in your own heart.

Paul learned contentment, as must every disciple of Jesus Christ. Contentment comes from choosing to remain in the truth that God has established and rejecting any message that contradicts that truth. Contentment is a choice. For the Christian husband, the truth is that God has given you and your wife to each other. Your choice is to be content with her:

- Who she is as a person
- Her intellect

- Her personality
- Her physical appearance
- Her spiritual gifts
- Where she came from (From God! Thank You, Lord!)

If you are not at peace or are discontent with your marriage because you and your wife are not walking in unity, that present discontent can be used by God to bring you and your wife to a place of renewed pursuit of God and each other.

But general discontent with your wife is not godly and is a potential inroad to your heart for sin, which will drive you further not only from your wife's heart but also from the heart of God. Regardless of why it's there, recognize discontent and take immediate action.

Don't allow yourself to live with discontent—even if it's compartmentalized to one area of your marriage. Either use that discontent as a positive catalyst to move you closer to God and to openly discuss with your wife important aspects of your marriage or reject it out of hand as an attack from the Enemy. Don't engage. With a spirit of discontent, there's no middle ground.

Reflection

- Have I allowed myself to live with a spirit of discontent toward my wife in any aspect of our marriage?
- Am I entertaining thoughts that lead me further toward discontent and away from the truth of what God has said?

Application

Positive messaging (especially if it's God's message!) is powerful. Tell yourself every morning,

- I'm content with my wife.
- She is God's gift to me! Thank You, Lord!

And tell your wife regularly,

- I'm content in our marriage. Thank you for being my wife.
- I love your body.
- I think you are beautiful.
- I am blessed by your walk with God.
- I love how intelligent you are.
- I appreciate all you do.

Prayer

God my Father, it's easy to see how discontent can get a foothold and take root in my mind. Lord, I pray that I would be vigilant against my own inclinations toward discontent and against the Enemy's attempts to speak lies into my mind and to call into question Your goodness to me. May this week be one in which I fill my wife's heart with confidence as I not only say but demonstrate that I am content with her, the most beautiful gift You've given me after salvation through Jesus Christ. In Jesus's name, amen.

25

Trials

The LORD is near to those who have a broken heart,
And saves such as have a contrite spirit.

Psalm 34:18 NKJV

The life of the believer is full of every kind of weather. Who wouldn't prefer clear skies, fair winds, and no worries? But that's not the path for anyone.

The writer of Ecclesiastes sums it up well:

To every thing there is a season, and a time to every purpose under the heaven: a time to be born, and a time to die; a time to plant, and a time to pluck up that which is planted; a time to kill, and a time to heal; a time to break down, and a time to build up; a time to weep, and a time to laugh; a time to mourn, and a time to dance. (3:1–4 KJV)

Have you traveled the hard, merciless road of adversity? Have you experienced the gaping wound of a heartache so severe that it cuts to the bone? There's no dancing on that road. Sometimes the pain runs so deep as to call into question the logic of going on, humanly speaking.

If you haven't been there yet, you can be certain such a season is appointed for you. If an unwelcome night hasn't yet closed in over you like the irresistible undertow of a giant wave, one day it will. At some point, the sky will turn menacing, and the cold, heartless hand of darkness will come to test the foundation and measure of your faith.

If God should ask you to face times such as Job faced, when crushing sorrow will press on your chest, how will you walk through them? Will you face heartache with self-focus or with faith and an open, understanding heart, alongside your wife?

When life gets this tough, it's natural to default to self-preservation: *What's happening to me? How am I feeling? What should I do? What do I need?* But you're the husband—the one who is to face such trauma and not lose sight of your bride. When life forces you to tighten your grip, make sure you don't let go of each other.

The only way to keep from the path of self-focus is to know, remember, and believe what God has said. Turn to Him in troubled times. "The LORD is near to those who have a broken heart, and saves such as have a contrite spirit" (Ps. 34:18 NKJV). Yes, He is near, and He saves. To have faith is to know what God has said and to believe it.

Remind yourself each day—before your ship leaves the harbor—that you are not facing this, feeling it, or walking alone. Your wife is there. You are one, and God is with you. Share your faith with each other during heartache. Don't retreat to the independence of your wounded soul. When you cut her out, you're hindering the Spirit's work in your home and marriage. Consider that your wife will either experience your turmoil, trauma, and doubt on her own, or she'll experience your peace, yielded brokenness, pain, and faith together with you. Your communion with God in the heartache, or its absence, will determine which it will be.

Reflection

- What is my natural response to dealing with trauma and heartache?
- Do I make my wife feel like I'm being vulnerable, walking with her and sharing my pain with her?
- Do I allow pain to isolate me from my wife?

Application

- Talk about trials with your wife. Discuss how you will walk through the next challenge together.
- Ask your wife to describe what would give her confidence that you are *together* in such circumstances.
- Remind yourself that you are to be leading in your relationship, and that leadership doesn't get put on hold because challenging things are happening.

Prayer

God my Father, I know that You require me to face many difficult challenges in life. No one escapes heartache. Help me to be the godly man and biblical leader in my marriage so that we will face together the things You ask us to, in the way you intend—with faith. May I love her deeply in life's deepest valleys because I am walking with You. In Jesus's name, amen.

26

Miracles

You are the God who does wonders; You have declared Your strength among the peoples.

Psalm 77:14 NKJV

Does "the God who does wonders" still do them? Will He reach down into the details of your life—of your marriage—and act?

Miracles are about power—God's power. The most prevalent category of miracles in the Bible is miracles over nature, over the created order. Whether it's creation itself (Gen. 1–2), the sun standing still for Joshua (Josh. 10:13), or oil for an old woman (2 Kings 4), miracles demonstrate that the power of nature is superseded by the power of God. When Jesus chided the disciples for their faithlessness as the boat was filling up with water, He spoke to the elements. One word, and the winds died and the waves dissipated (Matt. 8:27). That is power.

Some argue that miracles do not happen now and could never have happened because they violate the laws of nature, and everyone knows you can't break the law! But, as mathematician and Christian apologist Dr. John Lennox often explains, the laws of nature aren't unbreakable "laws" at all but mere descriptions of what we usually observe. It's rather a small matter for the Creator of the universe to intervene in His creation.

The purposes of miracles include blessing people, equipping servants for God's plan, judging enemies, and authenticating the person of Jesus Christ. But is God still at work in this way today?

Those who tell you that miracles don't happen anymore are revealing something about themselves, not about the work of God in the world. God is still the God who does wonders and who wields His power in the lives of His people. For instance, my son was born blind, confirmed over many months by doctors. But he received his sight instantly following prayer at a church meeting, with fifty witnesses present, much to the astonishment of his doctors the following week.

It's not that miracles have ceased, but many people have lost their capacity to see, their willingness to seek, and their faith to believe. Are you in need of a miracle in your life—in your marriage? Ask for it. Ask for it in detail, trusting your Father, who loves to give good gifts to His children. Sometimes we confuse our needs and our wants, which is why we must ask in faith but always according to His will, as Jesus did in the garden of Gethsemane. Even still, at times God chooses to answer "no" or "wait." Will you choose faith and trust when God deems presently unnecessary the miracle you thought was imperative?

The safest place to be is in the hands of the God of all power, who will always answer your prayers and requests for His miraculous intervention according to His loving will for you.

Reflection

- Am I living with the understanding that I serve the God of all power?
- Am I walking in confident faith that I am in God's hand, under His protection, and that He always chooses what is best for me?
- Do I believe God is a good Father who gives good gifts?
- Is there a miracle, an intervention, that I should be asking the Father for right now?

Application

- Review some of the miracles in the Old and New Testaments. Remind yourself of the power of God.
- Speak to your wife about the mindset God desires you to have regarding His power and ability to act.
- Ask God (according to His will) for the miracle you believe you need. Share it with your wife, if appropriate, and trust God for the results, giving thanks regardless of God's answer.

Prayer

God my Father, I believe in and trust in You. You are the God of all power, who loves me and invites me to walk in fellowship with You. At times it's difficult for me to believe—to have faith—when I've made a request to You, but I know You still do miracles. May I be an example of faith to my wife, and may I always remain worshipful and faithful regardless of how You choose to answer me. In Jesus's name, amen.

27

Kindness

Put on therefore, as the elect of God, holy and beloved, bowels of mercies, kindness, humbleness of mind, meekness, longsuffering.

Colossians 3:12 KJV

A kind person . . . is this what comes to your wife's mind when she considers the man she pledged her life to years ago? Was the husband she encountered this morning, last week, last month a kind man? Is this how she would describe you in an honest moment with a trusted friend?

We're quick to help an older woman struggling with her groceries or a neighbor with that last-minute project or just about any request anyone makes of us, even total strangers. And we should be kind to them. Kindness should characterize the Christian man's interactions with others. But these are the easy kindnesses to give, as they cost little and are generally given on our own terms.

For the Christian husband, there's another level of real kindness—that which has its source in the indwelling Holy Spirit. It's the kindness that is given daily and cheerfully to one's wife—a way of being that has no thought for itself but is offered with concern only for what she needs or may enjoy. Spirit-led kindness is love with shoes on, love that acts whether it's convenient or not.

Being kind in this way has nothing to do with how we appraise ourselves. It's about how the other person—your wife—experiences you. It's about how she feels after she has interacted with you.

As you consider your recent past, have you found yourself readily expressing consideration to a perfect stranger but reserving for your wife a less-kind version of yourself? It's natural to fall into this pattern, as we often take the most liberties with those we love the most. But the Christian husband isn't to live a "natural" life. There's nothing natural about the Holy Spirit indwelling you and the life of Christ being lived out through you each day.

Spirit-filled kindness is like an amazing investment plan in marriage. The dividends that typically come back to those who are kind are exponential. And though sometimes they don't come back or are delayed, God is still calling you to walk in the Spirit so this fruit is evidenced in your life, regardless of what anyone else chooses to do—even your wife. Choosing to walk in the Spirit is about obedience to God, not about getting a return for your good behavior.

For most Christian husbands who are in close fellowship with God and who exude kindness toward their wives, a return will come. Either way, you are walking in obedience to God, who will one day speak directly to you regarding the spiritual service others received from you.

Reflection

- Am I a kind husband? Does my wife experience kindness from me?
- What is my pattern of communication? Do I typically interact with her and others in kindness?
- Am I setting a good example of kindness in my home in the way I speak, by my countenance, and in what I do and how I do it?

Application

Ask your wife if she considers you to be kind to her—not in individual acts but as a general rule.

Remember that the fruit of the Spirit is not something you determine to do but who you are as a result of the Holy Spirit working in you. Exuding fruit of the Spirit is the result of abiding in Christ and remaining in fellowship with God throughout your day.

Prayer

God my Father, I want to grow and mature as a man of God. I see clearly that kindness as a fruit of the Spirit isn't something I do in my own power but is available as I walk with You. I pray that I will walk in your Spirit this week so I will interact with my wife according to the life of Christ in me. I pray that I will be a blessing to her this week, in Jesus's name, amen.

28

Anger

Do not be eager in your spirit to be angry,
For anger resides in the heart of fools.

Ecclesiastes 7:9 NASB

Giving way to anger is like running toward a high cliff with a firm grip on those who are present. You're plummeting over the precipice and you're taking everyone else with you.

The unyielding truth about anger is that it destroys everything it touches—especially your relationship with your wife.

No husband sets out to be a fool, but the man quick to give way to anger is a fool, according to the Bible. There is no place in a biblical marriage for this kind of angry outburst, and yet it's all too common in many Christian relationships. Is anger a part of your communication pattern in your marriage?

In seeking to justify an outburst of anger with one's wife, appealing to "the truth" is a common approach. After all, the truth is important, and you were just making your case for it! "I'm right and she is just wrong!" Well, congratulations. You win, again. But it's a victory never worth winning because, without exception, when you give way to anger in your marriage communication, you always lose far more than you gain.

More steam, less esteem . . . and eventually none at all. No wife slams the door of her heart in one single move. But gradually, each time she experiences your anger, she closes her heart until it's shut tightly against you. Aside from a miracle of God, no force on earth will pry it open.

The truth does not need to be conveyed by a loud, angry, sarcastic voice and an aggressive countenance. The Bible instructs you to speak the truth *in love* (Eph. 4:15). Genuine love lowers the volume and the barriers to your wife's heart, increasing her hearing capacity.

Fools tell themselves lies, justifying their anger. But there is no justification for angry outbursts against your wife. All it means is that you lack self-control, are prideful, are operating in the moment without regard to the future, and are determined to win at the cost of your relationship.

Nobody's will is going down without a fight, but you are God's man, indwelt by His Spirit, and you *can* banish anger from your marriage communication. And, what's more, you're the only one who can do it. God will never do for you what He has given you the instruction and the capacity to do. God has given you His Spirit, but you are called on by Him to act.

Reflection

- Have I communicated with anger toward my wife?
- What would she think? If I answered no to the first question, would she agree?
- What are trigger issues, circumstances, or points that I tend to respond to in anger?
- Am I hiding behind my "rightness" to justify my anger?
- Is this a sin in my life? Do I need to turn from it and ask God, and my wife, for forgiveness?

Application

- Believe that angry outbursts toward your wife are sins.
- Accept the truth: Your anger in communication is destructive—every time.
- Recognize that your anger (even anger you suppress) closes your wife's heart to you.
- Admit that anger is not something that is happening to you; it's a choice you are making—every time.
- Meditate on this truth: You have the power through the Holy Spirit to exercise self-control and say NO to the inclination to respond in anger.

Prayer

God my Father, how quick I am to justify my angry inter-actions, convinced of my own "rightness." Lord, may I be like King David, who said, "Your word I have hidden in my heart, that I might not sin against You" (Ps. 119:11 NKJV). Lord, I don't want to be a fool. Burn into my heart the truth of Your Word in Ephesians 4:15 in which You instruct me to speak the truth in love. Thank You that I am Your son. Help me to walk in communion with You in this matter of banishing anger and communicating with my wife in love. In Jesus's name, amen.

29

Hope

The LORD taketh pleasure in them that fear him, in those that hope in his mercy.

Psalm 147:11 KJV

Everything this world offers that we can put our hope in is an illusion.

The rulers of the earth put hope in their power, but in Psalm 2 we see that Jehovah God laughs at them, literally scoffs at the futility and stupidity of their opposition to Him and His infinite power. Such earthly power is eliminated in a moment by the breath of His mouth.

Others put their hope in their riches, but what does Jesus say of those who do? It's all but impossible for the rich to enter eternal life with God. In Mark 10:25, Jesus said, "It is easier for a camel to go through the eye of a needle, than for a rich man to enter into the kingdom of God" (KJV).

I once sat by the deathbed of a wealthy woman in her late nineties. Her nose began running, and when a tissue was pulled from a box and held near her nose, her dull eyes rallied strangely, suddenly sparkling and alive. A thin, rasping voice scratched out her concern: "Wait! Do I have to pay for that [tissue]?" She died soon after.

No, money won't save you or give you security. In fact, if you're rich, Jesus says it's unlikely you'll make it to eternity with Him.

Have you ever been tempted to hope in the false things of this world rather than the only One who can bring you real security in this life and make good on His promise for your eternal future? Everyone has been. It's what Satan did with Jesus in his grand opportunity to tempt the Messiah at His weakest physical moment. And this is exactly what your Enemy does to you too. He offers counterfeit hope in a world that is passing away . . . and he wants you to pass away with it.

This is where the fear of the Lord (believing what He has said and that He will follow through—then altering your life accordingly) and hope in His unfailing love come in. When the God of all creation delights in you, you're in the safest, most secure place that exists. Where is your confident hope?

Is your hope fixed on that which can never be moved or on things passing away?

A husband who lives in hope brings a lightness of spirit into the home, lifting the spirit of his wife. Your wife takes her cue from you. When your confidence in the Lord is settled and your hope resides in what He has done through the sacrifice of his Son, Jesus Christ, and on what He will do next, you're providing real leadership in your marriage and bringing a buoyant spirit into your home.

Reflection

- Am I living in a spirit of hope and exuding that hope to my wife?
- Do I truly fear the Lord? Or am I expressing fear of things, circumstances, and people?
- Do I genuinely believe what God has said and that He will follow through on what He has said? Am I quick to alter my life to conform to what He has said?
- Is my hope settled in God's unfailing love for my wife and me and in His plans for our future together?

Application

- Discuss with your wife where your hope truly lies.
- Appraise yourselves and ask if you have been tempted to hope in anything this world has to offer: money, security, power, the approval of humans.
- Remind yourselves that the unfailing love of the Lord—the Good Shepherd—and the promises of your Father, found in the Word, are the only legitimate, wise, and secure things on which to set your hope.

Prayer

God my Father, where else can I turn for my hope and future? You are the only sure reality, and I believe Your promises. Lord, I believe and trust in the gift of Your grace and the offer of Your mercy through the death, burial, and resurrection of Jesus Christ. Thank You for the shed blood of Jesus, who paid for all my sin and broke the power of sin in me. Lord, may I live in hope this week. May people see the love of Christ in me, and may my wife especially see today the hope I have in You. I love You, my Father. In Jesus's name, amen.

30

Honesty

Lying lips are abomination to the Lord: but they that deal truly are his delight.

Proverbs 12:22 KJV

It's natural to think of honesty on a sliding scale from unimportant matters to serious violations, depending on the topic and whether being honest about a particular matter collides with other values.

Take, for example, a husband's perception about what it takes to keep the peace in his marriage. It's here that oneness and true unity of spirit in marriage are sometimes compromised:

- *It's better if she doesn't know.*
- *What she doesn't know won't hurt her.*
- *If I told her, it would just create strife.*

- *She won't be hurt if we don't discuss it.*
- *I don't like the pressure she puts on me, so I'll leave out a few details and she'll never suspect it.*

You can say something that is true and still use it to tell a lie. Misleading is lying. And in each scenario listed above, the husband is thinking of himself and living as a separate, independent entity. This is not the biblical way, and it obstructs the path to the depth of relationship God intends for the two of you.

God desires that all His people be honest in their communication, and for the Christian husband it's a matter of even greater significance. There isn't another person this side of heaven with whom you are one in the sense God established for a man and his wife from the beginning. There can be no hidden places in your hearts. It's perfectly legitimate to withhold or conceal information from the impertinent inquisitiveness of an acquaintance but not from your wife. She was designed to be ever and always on the "inside" with you.

Are you ever tempted to withhold specifics from your wife to keep her from understanding exactly what you're doing, where you're going, or what you think? The mind immediately runs to the "big matters," like personal purity, but true honesty, by the biblical definition, involves everything in life between husband and wife, even smaller matters.

For example, has your wife ever disapproved of something you were determined to do, so you told her you were going out to take care of something else, when you were really using that errand to cover your true purpose—doing what you wanted—without her knowledge?

Being an honest man, by God's definition, is not about telling just the "technical" truth or carefully choosing words or selecting information you choose to share. The person who withholds, misleads, or deceives, who keeps something back in a hidden corner of life, is a liar, regardless of how he deceives himself or others into thinking he's truthful. No relationship can stand under the weight of such duplicity. In an environment where even a "small" dishonesty is seen as acceptable, the true oneness of marriage can never thrive. Dishonesty deemed small is actually hiding something huge—a spirit of independence from one's wife and a lack of integrity.

The Bible refers to the Lord as "the Father of lights, with whom there is no variation or shadow of turning" (James 1:17 NKJV). This is how a biblical marriage thrives: no shadows, just like your heavenly Father.

Reflection

- Have I, in any sense, hidden things from my wife and made excuses to myself that doing so was justified?
- Am I completely honest with her—even in the matters I think of as small?
- Are there any "shadows" in our marriage—anything that I am hiding or withholding from her?

Application

- Make a genuine assessment of your heart. Are you thoroughly honest with your wife?
- Identify the areas or ways of communicating with your wife, if any, that reveal you have been keeping part of your life hidden—even a small part—and living with an independent spirit.
- Be honest with your wife. Share with her your renewed purpose to walk openly together as one.

Prayer

God my Father, it's not difficult to know or understand that You require me to be honest. And yet, it's so easy to justify the times when being less than forthcoming seems okay—but it's not, and I know it. Lord, I pray for conviction to walk in integrity and openness with my wife. Help me to desire to please You and be obedient more than my flesh desires the easier path. May I lean on Your truth and not on my own logic or understanding. Father, I am Your son and Your servant, and I pray that my marriage reflects who I truly am. And may I love my wife this week, living as one with her in everything. In Jesus's name, amen.

31

Prayer

Praying always with all prayer and supplication in the Spirit, and watching thereunto with all perseverance and supplication for all saints.

Ephesians 6:18 KJV

An invitation to communicate with the God of the universe seems like an opportunity not to be missed. Which raises a question: Why do so few men pray?

What kind of a prayer life do you have? Would you encourage someone to follow your example in prayer? A life of consistent prayer—communication with the Father—can be an ongoing struggle.

In the context of war, an opposing force immediately endeavors to disrupt the communication channels of the army they face. Prevent communication between the command center and advanced units, and chaos shortly ensues. It's no different than what happens on the gridiron when players on the field don't know what their quarterback is doing. They cannot win. When you neglect prayer, your walk with God is similar. Spiritual success, growth, and security never follow silence between you and God.

Leading up to the passage above, we read that spiritual war is the context for the Christian life. To be successful in that war, a man must dress in the battle armor God provides. And then Ephesians 6:18 says this: "Praying always" (KJV).

Seen in the context of war, it's obvious why a soldier (you!) would be told to remain in communication with God. For equally obvious reasons, your Enemy, Satan, is determined to keep you from the very thing you are told to do. He's looking for a victory over you on the battlefield of your life.

What does it mean for you to pray always or pray without ceasing? It's hardly practical to pray 24/7. When would you sleep? And, no, the Word isn't instructing you to never stop actively praying a prayer. So, what is the heart of this admonition for the Christian man?

The essence of prayer is communication in fellowship with the Father. This instruction is about regular prayer but also about the posture of your heart to be inclined to communicate with the Father about anything, on a moment's notice.

Romans 12:12 instructs the faithful to be "instant in prayer" (KJV). This phrase means to be of ready mind, always inclined to turn to the Father. Constant readiness to seek Him at any moment of your day.

No Christian husband can lead his home successfully while neglecting fellowship with the Father through prayer. The God of the universe is calling on you to be in constant fellowship with Him. That's an amazing, favored position to be in.

You are at war against a determined Enemy. Not only is your constant communication with the Father an awesome opportunity, it's also critical for your success on the battlefield.

Reflection

- Have I allowed less important pressures, interests, and distractions to keep me from regular communion with God through prayer?
- What is the example I'm setting in my home?
- Would I honestly want my wife and/or children to follow my example of the last month?

Application

- Establish a regular time of prayer in the morning and guard it like a knight guarding the drawbridge of a castle.
- Purpose to remain in communion with God throughout the day.
- Be sure to regularly pray for your wife—for her needs and for God's blessing and leading in her life.
- Establish a regular time to pray with your wife.

Prayer

God my Father, thank You for always being there, instructing me to seek You. I've been inconsistent in my prayer life, but I also see that You're looking for far more than a prayer time that ends early in the day. You desire that I remain in communication with You at all times. Lord, may I walk in close fellowship with You this coming week, and I pray that I will be an example of a godly man who walks continually throughout his day with the God who created and loves him. Help me be that man this week and beyond. In Jesus's name, amen.

32

Purity

> Let no one despise your youth, but be an example to the believers in word, in conduct, in love, in spirit, in faith, in purity.
>
> 1 Timothy 4:12 NKJV

You can't live up to God's standard if you don't first know what it is and then believe you have been empowered by His Spirit to walk in it.

No one expects maturity and godliness in a young Christian man. No one except the God of the Bible. This is why the apostle Paul admonishes Timothy to "Let no man despise thy youth" (1 Tim. 4:12 KJV).

To our modern ears, this sounds a bit like something John Wayne might say to a young man: "Okay, son, I'm going to tell ya how to get on in life. Mark your territory and stand your ground." But this isn't John Wayne. It's God speaking by the Holy Spirit, through the apostle, teaching Timothy—and us—how we are to live.

Paul is telling Timothy, regardless of his relative youth, to live in such a way that no one could look at his behavior, choices, and speech and despise or dismiss him as young and immature. The description Paul gives in these verses is the description of the normal life of a biblical Christian man.

Be an example in how you speak, in your conduct, in how you selflessly love and care for others, in your inner thought life, in faith, in purity.

It's easy to agree with everything on that list in theory, but then there's that last one: purity. No sexual sin in your thought life or physical life, public or private. Does God really expect you to be an example of purity to everyone you encounter, at all times, and keep up that behavior when you are alone?

Who you are when no one is looking is who you really are.

Yes, God expects purity from His men—from you. How are you doing with that? Maybe you're avoiding the "big" sins—physical adultery, regular porn use, and so on—but what about in your spirit, in your thought life? Would you encourage others to follow your private example if they knew what really went on there? Every Christian husband should be able to say yes to that question.

God's standard for you is purity, as impossible as that may seem to your flesh. But you follow the Good Shepherd, and a powerful truth about Him is that the Good Shepherd never leads where the sheep cannot follow. Everyone in your world may tell you that you cannot truly follow God in His instruction for you to be pure—so pure that you are an example for others to follow. But your truth and instruction come from the Word, not the world.

The Enemy wants a church full of men who say, "Don't follow my example." God wants exactly the opposite. Will you be an example of purity this week to those you know and those who encounter you?

Reflection

- Have I been walking in purity in all things this week?
- Do I genuinely believe that purity in all things is God's standard for me?
- Do I believe that how God instructs me to live is also possible to attain?
- In what areas do I naturally struggle?

Application

- In your quiet time each morning, tell yourself that God's standard for the normal Christian life is purity in all things.
- Remind yourself that you are not weak. You are strong by the power of the Spirit who indwells you.
- List the areas in which you typically struggle.
- You have the power to say NO to sin. Discuss this truth with your wife.
- Cut out any behaviors that make you vulnerable to those things you find you are most susceptible to.

Prayer

God my Father, I confess that I am tempted to have a casual attitude about purity in some aspects of my life. I'm prone to step into the trap of thinking that some of these sins are minor and not that important, like stealing a glance at a pretty woman or entertaining a sensual or sexual thought for a short time. Please forgive me. Lord, I know You mean business with me, that You are a jealous God, as Your Word says, and that You will not share Your glory with another. You desire that I should grow and mature and that in my entire life I should give You the glory You deserve. I'm receiving Your Word, that I should walk in purity. Thank You for empowering me to do so by Your indwelling Holy Spirit. Father God, may I walk as You've called me to walk, starting right now. In Jesus's name, amen.

33

Goodness

But the fruit of the Spirit is . . . goodness.

Galatians 5:22 KJV

Every right-thinking husband desires to be good—to be thought of as a good man. Even among those who deny Jesus Christ are men who do things that are accounted by others as good.

Yet the perspectives of God and man on what is "good" are miles apart. Isaiah 64:6 declares that "all our righteousnesses [the good things we do before we belong to God] are as filthy rags" (KJV) in God's sight. How filthy? It's passed over in English translations, but the Hebrew word *iddah*—rendered "filthy" in our English translations—means "menstruation" or "the flow of menstruation." God compares the things we do to account for our own righteousness to a used menstrual cloth. Apart from God, no one can be good and, therefore, no one can do any good that will commend them to God.

Jesus agrees. In Matthew 19:16, a man approaches Him with a question about being good, saying, "Good Teacher, what good thing shall I do that I may have eternal life?" (NKJV). Immediately Jesus points out a problem in the man's thinking: "Why do you call Me good? No one is good but One, that is, God" (v. 17 NKJV).

Jesus wasn't saying of Himself that He was not good. Jesus is God incarnate, never sinned, and therefore was, is, and always will be good. The young man didn't understand this. He also didn't understand that Jesus was teaching him that he couldn't save himself by doing something good to earn eternal life.

The goodness God naturally expects from your life is not something you do to get something you want. Rather, it's the evidence of who you are—a man who has repented and received the free gift of God's grace and, consequently, has the Holy Spirit living in him. As the Word says, you (the redeemed) are the temple of the Holy Spirit (1 Cor. 6:19).

Do you believe that biblical truth—that you are indwelt by the Holy Spirit? Goodness is the natural expression of walking in that truth—you are good and do good because of the grace you have received and the life of Christ in you.

This kind of goodness, and the expressions of it that follow, come from a heart concerned with what's best for others—with what's best for your wife.

Is your life filled with goodness toward your wife? Not to get something but because of who you are in Christ?

Reflection

- Is the Spirit's fruit of goodness evident in my life?
- Does my wife see and experience this manifestation of the Spirit in the normal course of our life together?
- Are there areas of my life and communication with my wife where this goodness is absent?
- Specifically, in what areas of my interaction with my wife do I need to grow, mature, and yield my heart further to God so the Spirit's fruit of goodness is evident?

Application

- Set aside time to reflect or meditate on this matter of goodness (selfless consideration of what is best for others and, specifically, for your wife).
- Ask God to reveal where He would have you increase fruit in this area of your life.
- Humbly ask your wife for her perspective and input.
- Remember that this is about walking in the Spirit through communion with God because of who you are in Christ; it's not something you decide to do to get a desired response.

Prayer

God my Father, the closer I draw to You, the more the areas of my life that are not conformed to the image of Christ come into focus. I do want to be a good man by Your definition, and I understand that this isn't some special status of super-spiritual men but the normal life of a man yielded to You. Thank You for blessing me with my amazing wife. I pray that she increasingly experiences the goodness of the Spirit in my life as I walk in fellowship with You. I love you, Lord. In Jesus's name, amen.

34

Worship

But the hour cometh, and now is, when the true worshippers shall worship the Father in spirit and in truth: for the Father seeketh such to worship him. God is a Spirit: and they that worship him must worship him in spirit and in truth.

John 4:23–24 KJV

Every Christian will say that worship of God is important, but what does it mean to worship God? Do you worship God? And does your wife know you are a worshiper of God? If you were to make a list of what you do to worship God every day, what would be on it?

Many Christians today believe that worshiping God means thinking about Him and approaching Him in any positive way one desires. As we see in God's rejection of the sacrifice of Cain, that certainly wasn't true in the beginning. Centuries later, it wasn't true among the Israelites either. And it is not true today.

In the days of the Old Testament, followers of Yahweh were instructed about where (in the tabernacle and then in the temple) and how (by following Mosaic law) they were to worship. They were to approach and worship God by exacting standards and protocols. But when Jesus meets the Samaritan woman—at a time when worship is still taking place in the temple at Jerusalem and the Samaritans are still worshiping in their own way far from the temple—he tells her that God is seeking worshipers, but not just any worshipers. He's looking for specific kinds of worshipers: those who worship Him in a specific location and in a particular way. Jesus says to her, "But the hour cometh, and now is, when the true worshippers shall worship the Father in spirit and in truth" (John 4:23 KJV), indicating that all worship of God is about to change and that the true worshipers God is seeking will worship in spirit, regardless of their geographical location.

The true worship of God no longer has to happen in a building or in a place deemed sacred. It takes place in the spirit of the worshiper, who Jesus said would worship "in truth" (v. 23)—not in the convoluted mishmash of the Samaritans' defective worship, nor in the rites of Jewish worship. No, people born of the Spirit worship God in truth when the commitment of their heart and their acts of homage to God are directed and governed by God's Word.

Do we know what genuine worship is at its core? As with many Hebrew and Greek words, the word in the Bible rendered *worship* in English is somewhat elastic. But one dominant theme of that word is used overwhelmingly in the biblical text: to prostrate or bow down, to physically kneel with your face to the earth. To worship is to prostrate oneself before the object of one's worship.

This is exactly what we see all Israel doing at the dedication of the temple in 2 Chronicles 7—bowing their faces to the ground in worship while the glory of the Lord filled that place, as others do all throughout Scripture.

Do you worship the Lord in the biblical way? Worship is not something that is to take place only in a church. Biblical worship has nothing to do with a geographic location and can be done anywhere.

Do you regularly worship God in spirit . . . and in truth? Do you bow down before Him, prostrating yourself in homage to the God of Abraham, Isaac, and Jacob, to the God of all creation, the God who loved you and proved it by sacrificing His only Son so you might be reconciled to Him in true fellowship? Is He not worthy that you should prostrate yourself on the ground before Him in homage?

Worship God each day. Give the Lord His due.

Reflection

- Do I worship the Lord in my spirit and in truth, according to the Word?
- Have I given the Lord the reverence due Him?
- Does my wife know I worship God in reverence and holy fear?
- What example of worship am I providing for her?
- When was the last time I humbled myself to the ground before the Lord of glory?

Application

- Make a regular practice of prostrating yourself before the Lord.
- Talk with your wife about your commitment to worship God.
- Encourage her to regularly worship the Lord.
- Take time to praise the Lord together.

Prayer

God my Father, You are worthy of my praise and my worship. I bow before You to give You the homage due to You and to take my rightful place in Your presence. May I learn to love You more. Thank You for all You have done for me. Please help me to be an example to my wife of what it means to be a husband who worships You in spirit and in truth. In Jesus's name, amen.

35

Thankfulness

I thank my God always concerning you for the grace of God which was given to you by Christ Jesus.

1 Corinthians 1:4 NKJV

The concept of thankfulness is central to the life of a Christian. Over seventy times, the Word admonishes God's people to give thanks. God has showered His people with His good gifts, and we are instructed to give thanks regularly.

In speaking to the Corinthian church, Paul says that he repeatedly gives thanks to God for them and for a very specific reason—for the grace of God that was given to them when they became believers. The next few verses reveal that Paul is referring to the spiritual gifts they have received in abundance. He is exceedingly thankful for all they have received from God and for how these gifts can bless the church.

Although some strong correction follows later in this letter, at this point in the public reading, they must have been deeply gratified. To know that someone is always sincerely thanking God for you and the gifts that God has entrusted to you is greatly encouraging to hear.

Can you think of a reason to express thankfulness to God for someone? Who would God have you see in this same light—in Christ Jesus, filled with giftedness that is a deep blessing to you and others?

Your wife, of course! She and her unique God-given giftedness are God's gift to you. Does your wife experience you as a husband who regularly and genuinely gives thanks to God for her? And then tells her about it?

Paul makes a major point of stating openly to the Corinthians that he regularly tells God how grateful he is for them. It's not just how he feels internally. It's not a private matter between him and God. Paul is open and unreserved in his acknowledgment of them being in Christ and, as a consequence, of them being endowed by God with many spiritual gifts.

Your wife's heart needs to hear of your thankfulness to God for her, including that you see her spiritual giftedness and that you are specifically grateful for this incredible grace God has given her with which to bless you and your home.

Will this coming week be filled with your open, directly stated thankfulness for your wife?

Reflection

- Have I thought specifically about the spiritual gifts of my wife and the blessing they are to me? Do I know what these gifts are?
- When was the last time I expressed to her that I was giving thanks to God that she is in Christ and that she has been given these amazing spiritual gifts that are a blessing to me?
- Does my wife have an abiding confidence that I am expressive and open with God about how thankful I am for her?

Application

- Set aside some time this week to tell your wife that you are regularly giving thanks to God for her.
- Write down the specific gifts that she has been given by God and how they bless you and your home.
- Pray with her in the moment, giving thanks to God for her.

Prayer

God my Father, thank You so much for my wonderful wife. She is such a beautiful blessing to me. I'm deeply grateful for the ways You have equipped her with spiritual gifts not only for her to bless me with but also for Your use in the church. Lord, I pray that this week and the coming weeks will be filled with regular expressions from me directly to her of how thankful I am for the wife, spiritual woman, and friend that she is. Thank You, Lord. In Jesus's name, amen.

36

Holiness

But as He who called you is holy, you also be holy in all your conduct, because it is written, "Be holy, for I am holy."

1 Peter 1:15–16 NKJV

Really? I'm supposed to be holy, as God is holy?

Often we give up on being holy before we ever wrestle with how God has called us to walk. It's understandable. The concept of holiness is so foreign to our natural way of thinking, it seems all but inaccessible to the human mind. What exactly is God asking us as men, as husbands, to do?

James 1:22 reminds us that, more than merely hearing the truth of God's Word, we are to *do*—to take action: "But be ye doers of the word, and not hearers only, deceiving your own selves" (KJV). There is no holiness without obedience.

To be holy is to live set apart for God. Set apart from what? From your manner of life in the flesh, which was apart from God, described in 1 Peter 1:14 as "former lusts" (KJV). It's important that we don't overspiritualize, and consequently obscure, what God means for us to grasp.

Simply put, walking in holiness is saying NO to the world, your desires, and the devil in the matter of living for yourself. It is recognizing that you are set apart for God and His purposes right now in this present moment. When this is true, you are walking in holiness. You needn't worry about tomorrow, next week, or next month. God's priority is your exclusivity in the present moment of communion with Him. Stay in His presence, and tomorrow will take care of itself.

Holiness is not some misty, hyper-spiritual concept that is impossible to define and therefore to understand. That is how your Enemy wants you to think about it so you won't think about it at all and so you will dismiss it as impossible. Holiness is a thoroughly practical instruction about how you are to choose to walk in communion with God in the present moment.

And with this understanding, you properly come to realize that you are set apart exclusively to your wife, where the manifestations of all those God-given desires are to be satisfied. Walking in holiness results in oneness in your communion with God and with your wife.

Reflection

- Is there anything I've been doing that is unholy or leading me toward unholiness?

- Do I see myself as "set apart" for God—for His use, His blessing, His purposes?
- Would my wife say I am a holy man?
- If so, how would she define that?

Application

Are you walking in holiness with God at this moment? Walking in holiness means:

- Confessing your sin.
- Regularly reading the Word of God.
- Having a regular prayer life.
- Walking in purity: staying completely away from all the offerings of sexual sin, including physical, visual, and mental.
- Remaining in communion and fellowship with the Father.

If you are not walking in holiness with God, you can enter in right now, in this moment. First John 1:9 says, "If we confess our sins, he is faithful and just to forgive us our sins, and to cleanse us from all unrighteousness" (KJV).

Remember, holiness is walking in communion with God.

Prayer

God my Father, there are so many things in this world designed to distract me, trip me up, and cause me to fall. Yet You call me to be holy, and I see now that to be holy isn't some impossible-to-attain state of superspirituality but a matter of day-to-day practicality. I want to grow and mature. I desire to walk in obedience to Your Word, to be holy as You call me to be. But I know this can only happen by the power of the Spirit that indwells me and by my conscious choice to walk in that power. Lord, help me to be sensitive to the Spirit's promptings, to be watchful and quick to say no to the temptations that I face. And help me to live out an example of holiness with the wife You have blessed me with. In Jesus's name, amen.

37

Grace

Let your speech always be gracious, seasoned with salt, so
that you may know how you ought to answer each person.

Colossians 4:6 ESV

In an age of willful lies in politics and media, cancel culture,
and the in-your-face belligerence of so much of social media,
speaking *without* grace has become a given in society.

If you were required to come up with examples of when
you spoke with a lack of grace to someone, would you have
to scour your memory for a rare incident, or would your mind
race to a recent encounter? For many, memory serves up several
not-too-distant examples.

Are you a husband of grace or the lack thereof in communication with your wife?

A lack of grace in speaking is a function of many things: personality (some are naturally more confrontational or contrary than others), upbringing (some are poorly trained in good manners), and being led by one's flesh rather than by the Spirit when responding to others.

There's no lack of justification for being ungracious in a given circumstance. Somehow, in our minds, those reasons absolve us for how we communicate. But God doesn't care about our reasons, however normal and justified we think they are. In fact, the Bible ignores altogether the reasons we may have for being ungracious in our speech. It's not important why you spoke that way. It is important that you grow and mature and become obedient to the instruction of how to speak to others . . . starting with your wife.

The shocking reality of the New Testament is that wherever behavior is called upon for change—from what the Bible calls "walking in the flesh" to walking in the Spirit—the responsibility for living out that change is given to the individual. It's on you. God empowers you through the Holy Spirit, equips you through His armor, and makes provisions for each encounter, not allowing you to be tempted beyond what you are able to withstand.

The soft-sounding "*Let your speech* always be gracious, seasoned with salt" (Col. 4:6 ESV) is actually an imperative statement. It can be translated: "Ensure that you speak with grace at all times. Cultivate this quality in all your communication."

Why? So you will know how to "answer each person" (Col. 4:6 ESV). This includes your communication with your wife, the person you have more opportunity to answer than anyone else. The Bible makes it clear. You are always representing God with your mouth.

The husband who walks with God will cultivate this manner of speaking with grace *at all times* so that when he speaks with his wife, her experience will be that she is being spoken to with grace—all the time.

We tend to take the most liberties with those to whom we are the closest. What is your wife's experience? Is she living in the blessing of your obedience to this biblical injunction to speak with grace? If not, let this be the week she begins to enjoy the fruit of your obedience to God's Word when it comes to the matter of speaking with grace to her *at all times*.

Reflection

- What has been my wife's experience in this matter over the last month? Do I speak to her with grace at all times?
- Looking back on when I've been ungracious in communication, what were the triggers that I responded to in the flesh?
- Have I been, consciously or unconsciously, using my personality as an excuse to be ungracious in my speech?

Application

- Start your day with prayer on this matter.
- Remember that you are instructed by God to speak with your wife only in a gracious manner, always.

- If there are specific moments when you were ungracious with your wife, go to her, identify your sin without reference to anything she may have done or said, and ask her to forgive you for your sin against her.
- Are there times when you are most inclined to be ungracious? Do they tend to be when you are hungry, tired, or frustrated? Take stock and understand yourself and the tendencies of your flesh. Don't make excuses. Take responsibility. Seek God's help in being vigilant against the outbursts of your flesh.

Prayer

God my Father, it's easy to identify the recent times when I've not spoken with grace to my wife. Please forgive me and help me communicate to her that You have put Your finger on this aspect that You want changed in my communication with her. Lord, help her to receive my sincere apology and my request for forgiveness. May I go forward in the power of the Spirit to speak to my wife with grace at all times, representing You and Your kingdom well to her. In Jesus's name, amen.

38

Peacemaker

Blessed are the peacemakers,
For they shall be called sons of God.

Matthew 5:9 NKJV

Few circumstances are better designed to challenge peaceful interactions than bringing together two completely different people of opposite sexes and personalities, who have different levels of maturity and knowledge, different upbringings, and different life experiences. In a word: marriage. It's tailor-made for many unpeaceful moments throughout the days, months, even years.

Isn't it amazing how quickly you can find yourselves at odds? One moment everything is warm and close, and then boom! A disagreement arises and you're at odds with each other. The good news is you don't have to guess where contention in your marriage comes from. The Bible makes it very clear. Proverbs 13:10 says, "Only by pride cometh contention" (KJV). And when you remember that it's impossible to have an argument with a humble person, suddenly your part in that last dustup with your wife is illuminated: You were prideful. No peace can thrive there.

If there's only periodic peace in your marriage, punctuated by sessions of tension and being at odds, a big part of the problem of that repeated sin is your relationship with God.

Even though many marriages experience regular strife, the Word admonishes every Christian to pursue peace in relationships—that includes peace in marriage, and peace requires a peacemaker, which is easy to confuse with a peacekeeper. The peacekeeper will do whatever it takes to avoid difficulty and dodge conflict. This person is only stuffing feelings and preventing maturity in himself and his wife. The peacemaker doesn't avoid trouble but moves toward the conflict and deals with disagreement by gently seeking God's perspective, not his own agenda. The peacemaker seeks reconciliation so fellowship can be restored.

We tend to think of being a peacemaker as a gifting or personality trait, but the biblical perspective is that every believer is to be a peacemaker. Peace, Galatians 5:22 says, is a manifestation of the Spirit in one's life, not a spiritual gifting distributed to some but not others.

When Jesus gives the Sermon on the Mount, He starts with the eight blessings, known as the Beatitudes, and says, among other things, "Blessed are the peacemakers" (Matt. 5:9 KJV). Studying these first verses of Matthew 5 quickly reveals that Jesus isn't speaking of eight types of super-spiritual people but eight character qualities of a believer living a sanctified life.

Being a peacemaker is the natural character of a man yielded to God.

To be a peacemaker in your marriage is to walk with God, which will give you spiritual eyes to see conflict from God's perspective and the motivation to make every effort for both parties—you and your wife—to yield to God's priority of love and fellowship, even when you see things differently.

Reflection

- Is my relationship with my wife peaceful?
- Am I a peacemaker in my marriage?
- How is God asking me to change and grow?
- Have I led well, or do I need to acknowledge to my wife a deficiency in my pursuing a peaceful marriage and tell her how I intend to change?

Application

Ask your wife the following questions:

- Do you feel at peace with me today? What about last week? Last month?
- What have I done that has contributed to the peace in your heart?
- What have I done that has brought a lack of peace into our marriage?

- Can you think of something I could do that would increase the peace in our marriage? (And, husband, be sure to offer your thoughts about the change God is seeking in this aspect of your marriage.)

Prayer

God my Father, I know You are the God of peace and that You desire my wife and me to walk in peace together, before You. Please identify anything in my life that contributes to a lack of peace in our marriage. Help me to care for my wife's heart by humbly walking with You, by being in true fellowship and communion with You that I might walk in Your Spirit this week and live lovingly and peacefully with my wife. Lord, help me to eagerly seek peacemaking in our marriage. Give me wisdom to be sensitive to her needs and feelings, that I might be a blessing to her and together we might be a faithful example to others. In Jesus's name, amen.

39

Covenant

I have made a covenant with my eyes;
Why then should I look upon a young woman?

Job 31:1 NKJV

To enter into a covenant—a solemn agreement to which you commit to be bound—is serious business because the fulfillment or dissolution of that covenant is based on integrity. The agreement has been made, but will the parties follow through? There are many different kinds of covenants, including marriage—the covenant you entered into on your wedding day.

As a faithful man on the appointed day, you desired for your wife to understand and hear in the presence of witnesses that her heart could safely and completely trust in you "until death do you part."

Although the ceremony and the vows are common in Christian churches, it's equally common to hear Christian men speak of their eyes as if they are a separate, independent intelligence they have no control over: "I just can't control my eyes." But there are two persons who will never be convinced of this claim: your wife and God—and for good reason. It isn't true.

A husband's eyes do not operate independently of his mind. Yes, eyes see things unintentionally, but engaging with those random scenes is another matter. Eyes look where they are directed to look by the mind. No man is responsible for what randomly appears in front of him, but every man is responsible for engaging his mind with that image or person. Every man is responsible for where he chooses to look.

As long as a husband has convinced himself he is a victim of what his eyes are doing, nothing will change. Why would it? He's not responsible for what's happening. Such is the power of misinformation. The power isn't in the truth or falsehood of the information but in the belief one has in it.

Job had made a covenant with his eyes to ensure his integrity in marriage. He would not lust after another woman because he would never look at another woman with lust. He made an agreement—a solemn commitment—with his eyes that he would never use them to sin.

Perhaps you've settled the issue of lusting visually and won this battle for good, as Job indicates he has, and that is excellent if you continue to walk in humility and close fellowship with the Father. If you haven't, the Father desires that you understand and accept the responsibility and power you have to direct your eyes and protect your thoughts in order to live within the covenant you have made.

The husband who has made a covenant and lives in it is walking in the path of blessing, and in so doing is blessing the woman he is walking with in this life.

Reflection

- Do I accept that I am responsible, all the time, for where my eyes rest and what I allow into my thoughts?
- Have I settled the issue, once and for all, that any degree of "looking" is a violation of my marriage vows?
- Do I truly acknowledge the power I have to bless or bring destruction to the heart of my wife by how I conduct myself with respect to my eyes?

Application

- Embrace a zero-tolerance policy for looking with lust at anything or anyone besides your wife. It's never okay under any circumstances. Your eyes are for your wife only.
- Remind yourself that you have entered into a covenant. Live as a man of integrity to that covenant.
- Practice looking away.

Prayer

God my Father, I, like Job, am making a covenant with my eyes to never purposefully look at another woman or image, or anything that would dishonor my vows to my wife. I desire to honor You and my wife all the days of my life. Surely, the Enemy will continue to go around like a roaring lion seeking to devour me, but I know that You have given me the strength to resist and, consequently, to stand against any temptations that come my way. Thank You for the power of Your Word. Lord, I pray for protection over my marriage. In Jesus's name, amen.

40

Remembering

Remember the former things of old: for I am God, and there
is none else; I am God, and there is none like me.

Isaiah 46:9 KJV

There are few instructions in the Bible repeated more often
than the admonition to remember. It seems that God's
people need constant reminding. Everyone can remember God
and our need for Him, His help, His care, and His provision
when times are bad. But when the season of favor and blessing
is extended, how easy it is to drift away from the heart of God.

Aside from the rainbow, God puts the responsibility on His
people to maintain the memory of Him. God instructs and
then expects us to take steps to remember. How can we forget
His mighty acts, His great love, His steadfast care so soon? Are
symbols of remembrance really that necessary? God thinks so.

In Joshua 4, God establishes His priority for His people to remember.

> This shall be a sign among you; when your children ask later, saying, 'What do these stones mean to you?' then you shall say to them, 'That the waters of the Jordan were cut off before the ark of the covenant of the LORD; when it crossed the Jordan, the waters of the Jordan were cut off.' So these stones shall become a memorial to the sons of Israel forever." (vv. 6–7 NASB)

And at the Last Supper, Jesus looked at the Twelve and said of the bread, "This is my body which is given for you: this do in remembrance of me" (Luke 22:19 KJV). The Lord's Supper is many things to many different religious traditions, but in every tradition, it includes remembering what Jesus Christ has done for the world on the cross and for each of us personally. We're prone to forget, so we're told to remember.

In every Christian marriage, the milestones of God's hand of favor and goodness are many and varied. You exchanged vows and rings at your wedding, but can you think of moments in your marriage worthy of establishing symbols of remembrance?

Careening through a hectic life can leave all those important, powerful, beautiful moments obscured by the dust of time. But remembering is important and will keep you grounded in times when life seems bent on calling all that goodness into question. Your Enemy's focus is to call into question the goodness of God, as he did in the garden of Eden. Symbols of remembrance in your marriage are for you as time marches on, but they're also for those who come after you—like the twelve stones were at the Jordan River crossing—reminding future generations of the goodness of the God their fathers and mothers served.

Reflection

- When has God directly blessed my life, both when I was single and since I've been a married man?
- What are some of the principal milestones in our marriage that should never be forgotten?

Application

- Set aside a time this week (or establish a time when you both can focus) to discuss with your wife the importance of remembrance and how to be proactive against the forces of modern life that leave no room for such reflections.
- Record with your wife the many times God has been good to you—and be specific.
- Together, give thanks for all that is on that list.
- Discuss with your wife symbols of remembrance that you could acquire or make and places you might put them in your home.

Prayer

God my Father, thank You so much for how good, gracious, and loving You have been to me and my wife over the years. I see the priority You put on symbols of remembrance in the Old Testament and Jesus Christ's admonition to remember with broken bread and poured out wine what He has done for us on the cross. We have been truly blessed. Lord, may I be a faithful husband before You, my God, as I lead my wife in establishing times and symbols of remembering Your goodness to us. In Jesus's name, amen.

41

Generosity

One man gives freely, yet grows all the richer;
  another withholds what he should give, and
    only suffers want.
A liberal man will be enriched,
  and one who waters will himself be watered.

Proverbs 11:24–25 RSV

Truly generous people never seek to make the recipient feel the cost of their gift.

What have you been given by a generous God? Salvation through the work of Jesus Christ on the cross. That's a great starting point for cultivating an open, generous spirit of blessing in marriage. You have not only been given much but you have also been given much to give to others, starting with your wife.

But our natural state apart from God invites a sort of careful mental bookkeeping in marriage where the squint-eyed soul peers endlessly between the "him" and "her" columns, attempting to balance the books. If you're not careful, it's easy to begin to feel like things are far out of balance, like your gifts are going unaccounted for.

If you desire your marriage to be a 50/50 deal, you will surely achieve that goal—you'll give 50 percent and get nothing more. But God has far more for the husband who chooses selfless generosity. When it comes to blessing others, the Word states the impossibility of "outblessing" someone else. In God's accounting, it is the generous giver of blessings who is himself blessed. "It is more blessed to give than to receive," we read in Acts 20:35 (KJV). Why is this? Because no act done out of genuine, selfless love goes unaccounted for by God Almighty.

The generous husband is not looking carefully at his ledger of gifts, favors, and care to ensure that he's not blessing his wife too much or too often. If you seek to shower your wife with blessing, without strings, expectations, or a call for reciprocation, you'll find that she will return to you that blessing, with interest.

And if you're experiencing a rough patch in your relationship, where consistent, loving blessing of your wife is unanswered, just remember that genuine, selfless blessing is never unaccounted for by God, who has promised to reward, in His time, generosity of all kinds given in love.

Reflection

- Am I operating from a spirit of generosity toward my wife?

- Do I typically seek blessing to flow from my wife to me or from me to my wife?
- Do I regularly bless my wife without keeping track of what I believe I should receive in return?
- In what ways could I generously give to bless my wife this week?

Application

Have a conversation with your wife and ask her, "What can I give to bless you this week?" Write down the ways she answers this question.

Resist the temptation to pat yourself on the back for your generosity to your wife, and resist the expectation of something in return.

Prayer

God my Father, I desire the marriage that You envisioned for us even before we were married. To move toward that goal, I know that I must have a selfless, Holy Spirit–inspired generosity and seek to regularly shower my wife with sincere, love-inspired blessing. Lord, I ask for wisdom, insight, and creativity to bless my wife in ways that show true, godly generosity. In Jesus's name, amen.

42

Cherish

Husbands, love your wives, even as Christ also loved the church, and gave himself for it; that he might sanctify and cleanse it with the washing of water by the word, that he might present it to himself a glorious church, not having spot, or wrinkle, or any such thing; but that it should be holy and without blemish.

Ephesians 5:25–27 KJV

It would be difficult to make the teaching in Ephesians 5 more absolute. Consequently, it's also difficult to make it more offensive than it already is to our modern sensibilities. It's not hard to understand; it's just challenging to accept.

But, as a Christian husband, you are responsible for what God instructs you to do, and this passage ensures that all Christian husbands have more than enough to keep them busy.

What you should be concerned about is the business God has with you—the instruction He has given specifically to you. All Christian husbands agree they should love their wives. But in what particular way are you to love yours? What are the specifics?

It's straightforward: The way Jesus loves the church, His bride, is the way you are to love yours! *Love your wife . . . even as Christ loved the church and gave Himself for her.* This instruction is more extreme than that which is given to wives. Your wife is instructed to submit to you, an imperfect man. You must love her, an imperfect woman, *perfectly*—as Christ did when He loved the church and gave everything for her.

You've got a lot of work to do. To love as Jesus loves? How exactly are you to do that? It's going to take some personal reflection and some supernatural intervention.

The principal focus, the number-one job you have, is to embody Christ's love for His church in your love for your wife so that anyone who sees your marriage can see God's love for the world in your marriage. Your priority isn't the local church, your job, those extra ministries the church has you involved in— not even your kids. Your wife is your principal focus because God has made her your priority.

The church and its mission—the Great Commission—are what Jesus is doing in the world. Loving your wife is what you are called to do in the world. This doesn't mean you can't do other things and don't have other roles to play in the local church, but your priority is to love her as Christ loves because God made it so. Is your wife the most cherished woman she knows?

Is this your mindset? Is this your perspective? When a man takes seriously the instruction of God to truly love his wife to this degree, he is creating a beautiful, safe place for her to fulfill her calling in the marriage.

Reflection

- Have I embraced the depth of the teaching I've been given regarding my wife?
- Do I lay down my life for her, or have I been selfishly guarding my own priorities?
- What are some things I can change to better reflect the requirement I have been given to love her as Christ loves the church?

Application

- Discuss with your wife the portion of the above Scripture that relates directly to you.
- Communicate to her that you desire to be the kind of husband described there.
- Ask her if she feels cherished by you, and explore the things that build or diminish this in her.

Prayer

God my Father, Your standard of behavior for me in my marriage seems completely overwhelming. How can I do it? I know I can't in my own strength. But I also know that for whatever You instruct, You also provide a way for me to be obedient. Your Holy Spirit is living in me that the life of Christ should be seen in me. As Galatians 2:20 says, "I am crucified with Christ: nevertheless I live; yet not I, but Christ liveth in me" (KJV). Lord, I have a long way to go, but I want to have the marriage You intend for me so I can be the example You desire of me. I pray that I will walk this out this week with my wife. Please protect our marriage from the Enemy as we seek to walk in obedience. And help us to stay focused on Your priorities. In Jesus's name, amen.

43

Trauma

Fear not, for I am with you;
Be not dismayed, for I am your God.
I will strengthen you,
Yes, I will help you,
I will uphold you with My righteous right hand.

Isaiah 41:10 NKJV

We know God is good. We know God is love. And we know the Bible is true. Even so, when tragedy strikes close to home, it's difficult to feel that the Father has your best interests in view, let alone a positive purpose in it all. What is the value, the purpose and meaning, of tragedy and loss?

Why did this have to happen? Wouldn't it have been better if . . . ?

There are times in life when the values of heaven and those of earth collide. What we deem pointless, painful, and tragic,

God considers important and useful in the work He continues to do for us and through us.

Even when you can't see things God's way or when it feels as if you can't see at all through the darkness of loss, God remains faithful, asking you to trust Him with your trauma. Without faith, tragedy is merely pointless pain in a meaningless universe.

One unmistakable truth Job discovered when everything he valued was ripped from him was that he was not in control. It's a lesson the loving Father desires that all His children learn. No one is the master of their own destiny. If they were, life wouldn't include tragedy and loss. Given ultimate decision-making power, we would never choose the hard road of loss and bereavement for ourselves.

But God, the decision-maker, does allow these things to overtake His children from time to time. Despite the worst the Enemy is allowed to throw at you, God remains in charge and at work in those very things. It's a truth difficult to accept.

God's plans and purposes in the tragedy of loss always extend far beyond what your feelings allow you to see. But dealing with tragedy doesn't mean you should deny how you feel. Jesus didn't. When He received the news that His friend Lazarus had died, Jesus wept. Even knowing the power of God, Jesus entered into the genuine emotion of loss and grief. And so should you if the moment of loss comes (perhaps it already has).

And in facing that loss, embrace your wife, draw near, and choose to be close—it's a time when oneness is as important as it is powerful. She'll need the strength of your arms then, and the truth is, you'll surely need hers as well. Grieve together and never let go of the truth that your heavenly Father, Jehovah God, is love, even when—perhaps especially when—you don't understand why tragedy was allowed to touch you.

Reflection

- Have I faced tragedy yet maintained faith in God's goodness and care? When my faith was tested, did it remain strong?
- If I have not yet faced tragedy on this scale, am I prepared to lead my wife through a season of loss and tragedy with understanding and unwavering faith in God—and by drawing closer to each other?
- Am I willing to grieve with my wife instead of pulling into myself?

Application

- Discuss with your wife the faith God desires you to have when you face tragedy together.
- Commit to the goodness of God regardless of the badness of the tragedy.
- Commit to drawing near to each other and grieving together rather than pulling apart into the solitude of your own pain.

Prayer

God my Father, Your Word has made it very clear that just because I follow You, I'm not guaranteed an easy life, free from tragedy and loss. Lord, I desire to lead well. I desire to hold on to You in the storm and to be near my wife so we might face life's hardest tests together and come out the far side having held on to our faith. Father, I know the only place faith can be tested is in the face of adversity. I certainly don't want to experience tragedy and loss, but I pray that You will find me faithful and steadfast if You decide to allow such a test in my life. And, Lord, help me to be strong and loving and a comfort to my wife should we be called on to face such things together. In Jesus's name, amen.

44

Gentleness

But the wisdom that is from above is first pure, then peaceable, gentle, and easy to be intreated, full of mercy and good fruits, without partiality, and without hypocrisy.

James 3:17 KJV

If I have yielded to the Spirit and allowed Him to do His work in me, gentleness naturally marks how I interact with my wife.

You might have to read that again. The thought arrests our attention because though we desire to be known as good husbands and we think of ourselves as godly men, in many Christian marriages, gentleness is about as common as snow in Florida. What place does gentleness have in your communication with your wife?

When the sky is blue and there's a nice warm breeze, we can be gentle all day long. But when the horizon darkens and the winds of challenge or trouble begin to blow (sometimes coming from our wives), are we gentle then? Gentleness is easy when there's no opposition, but gentleness that results from the Spirit's work in one's life doesn't yield to adverse conditions in marriage.

As men, we can chafe a bit at the idea of being gentle. Doesn't gentleness in a man reveal weakness of spirit? Isn't gentleness at odds with masculinity? Real manhood is tough, strong. Gentleness is a more feminine quality, more natural to women, right?

This is where cultural norms and biblical truth meet and you have to make a decision: Will you be a biblical, Christian husband? If the answer is yes and you are walking in the Spirit, you'll speak and act with gentleness toward your wife.

When we yield to the Spirit, the resulting gentleness carries with it an unexpected outcome in your marriage: a power that manifests itself in consideration and self-control. The husband walking in gentleness has created a safe place for his wife to open her heart to him.

Is gentleness, manifested by the presence of the Spirit in your life, characteristic of your interaction with your wife?

Reflection

- Ask your wife the following questions:
  - What things do I do that lack gentleness?
  - What things do I do that are gentle and bless you?
- Ask yourself the following questions:
  - Am I seeking God every day by reading the Word and praying—by staying in communion with Him throughout the day?
  - Does gentleness as a fruit of the Spirit flow from me into our marriage?

Application

Remember, gentleness that results from the life of Christ in you isn't about something you do but about who you are as you walk in communion with God.

Remind yourself that a lack of gentleness (especially in marriage) is a fellowship killer. First John 1:7 says, "But if we walk in the light, as he is in the light, we have fellowship one with another, and the blood of Jesus Christ his Son cleanseth us from all sin" (KJV).

This week, listen to the Spirit and yield to His promptings when you feel your words and tone getting edgy. Put down your right to react without gentleness. Pray in that moment that you will interact with your wife according to who you are in Christ.

Prayer

God my Father, I feel the rebel yell welling up in me often. Lord, help me to listen only to Your voice. I pray my flesh will lose every battle this week. I know You have empowered me by Your Spirit to walk in obedience to You. I desire to be Your son, to walk with You in true communion and fellowship today. I pray You would do Your refining work in me. You created me to live my life in the Spirit that I might be a strong but gentle husband, as You desire me to be. May I be a blessing to my wife today as I love her with gentleness. In Jesus's name, amen.

45

Money

For where your treasure is, there will your heart be also.

Matthew 6:21 KJV

The person who loves money is someone who doesn't understand its real value. For that, one need only look at the Bible's description of heaven. Revelation 21:21 reveals the proper value of gold: pavement. In heaven, gold is what they walk on.

The problem with wanting riches and spending one's life in pursuit of wealth isn't so much the greed of the person wanting more and more, although that is a problem. The real tragedy is not that the person is trying to get so much but that they're willing to settle for so little.

Jesus warns that your heart and your treasure will never be separated; if it's money that a person treasures, he can expect only to remain on earth when it's being devoured by fervent heat in the end times. There's no getting away from your pile of pavement then. This is why Jesus says it's almost impossible for a rich man to enter the kingdom of heaven (Matt. 19:24). Whatever someone spends their life grasping will return the favor and grasp their heart to the bitter end.

There's no room for Jesus Christ in a heart where money is improperly valued. God is hardly subtle on the matter. He'll tolerate no rivals. "For I the LORD thy God am a jealous God" (Exod. 20:5 KJV), we've been warned, which may be the reason Jesus talked more about money than any other subject. When it comes to the relationship between the Christian's worship of God the Father and their use of money, He wants His people to get it right.

The Bible's placing so much emphasis on the kingdom mindset regarding money should give us a clue about how important and dangerous our view of money can be in marriage. Is it any wonder that money is vying for first place among the reasons Christian couples get divorced?

We can mouth the words "It's all God's!" but is this true in our hearts? How is money handled in your marriage? Have you and your wife come together to discuss God's priorities, embraced a kingdom mindset regarding money, and laid your goals, and your gold, at His feet?

Reflection

- What is my view of money? Is it biblical, or do I love money and look at it as "mine," giving a little to God from time to time?
- Are my wife and I on the same page with our perspective, goals, and plans to achieve those goals?

- Do I treat the money we have the same way I expect my wife to treat it?

Application

- Establish the view that will govern money's presence in your home. Write down a few sentences that state your view of money.
- Receive the warning not to love money. Your love is for God, your wife, and family.
- Meet with your wife and establish what you will do with your income. How much will you save? How much will you give to the Lord's work? How much will you spend on life's necessities? How much will you spend on life's wants?

Prayer

God my Father, I pray that I would love what You love. I know that loving money is forbidden and brings real destruction to one's life. Yet money is a necessity, and You call me to be a steward of the resources I am entrusted with. Lord, I ask for Your blessing, for Your favor, and for Your wisdom in handling money. Please forgive me for the mistakes I have made with money and help me to listen to Your Spirit in handling money in the future. In Jesus's name, amen.

46

Faithfulness

So then, they are no longer two but one flesh. Therefore what
God has joined together, let not man separate.

Matthew 19:6 NKJV

A faithful man, who can find?

Proverbs 20:6 KJV

God's call on your life is to be a faithful man at all times,
in all things. Yet, when it comes to faithfulness with our
bodies, our time, our eyes, and our minds, we tend to be very
happy with improving percentages.

I only looked at porn once this week!

*I've really cut down on looking at other women when I'm
at work!*

I don't fantasize about other women nearly as much as I used to!

Are reduced sins, improving statistics, or lower percentages of unfaithfulness things to celebrate? Let's ask your wife. But that's not necessary, is it? You already know the truth. You and your wife both know that there's no meaning or value in partial faithfulness. Partial faithfulness has another name: unfaithfulness.

The only faithfulness that matters in marriage is total faithfulness. Being faithful to God and your wife isn't about improving on a scale from bad to better.

Jesus Christ didn't die on the cross for your incremental moral improvement. He did it for your total transformation. To clarify the issue, the Bible stipulates exactly how much sexual sin is acceptable among God's people: "But fornication, and all uncleanness, or covetousness, *let it not be once* named among you, as becometh saints" (Eph. 5:3 KJV).

Not once. Absolutely no sexual sin of any kind, ever, not even once, marks the normal life of a biblical, Christian man. The phrase "let it not be once named among you" means the same as "see that it doesn't happen." This Scripture is saying that you are responsible for the outcome in this matter of the frequency of sexual sin in your life.

Are you a faithful man? Can your wife trust you, unequivocally, explicitly, regardless of where you are, day or night, at all times? If you fear God, you will never be found in places or doing things you would be ashamed to have your wife discover by chance.

Total faithfulness to God and your wife—a pipe dream, or the call of God on your life? The awesome truth for a man who desires to be faithful in all things is that you have to concern yourself only with the moment you are in. Are you in fellowship with the Father right now?

Instead of getting caught up in an endless theological argument about the impossibility of a life of perfection (which *is* impossible this side of heaven for all but Jesus Christ) and using that argument as cover for the sinful choices you make, let's focus on the moment you're in right now. And in this moment, you can be a faithful man in perfect communion and fellowship with your heavenly Father, with whom you have been reconciled through Jesus. Enter in and remain.

Reflection

- In honesty before God, have I been a faithful husband in every aspect of my life, in public and in my private life and thoughts?
- Is God putting His finger on areas of my life in which I have not been faithful?

Application

If you have been walking in faithfulness, humbly praise the God who makes you strong by the power of His Spirit in you. Look into your wife's eyes and tell her you are her faithful man and that she never has to worry or wonder if you're being faithful to her, even in your thought life.

If you've been unfaithful at any level, repent before God, asking His forgiveness. And remember, the word *repent* means "to turn from." True repentance is to turn from your sin. Find a quiet moment to repent, and then ask forgiveness of your wife.

Believe the truth! First Corinthians 10:13 is a *power verse!* Memorize it and walk in its truth:

> There hath no temptation taken you but such as is common to man: but God is faithful, who will not suffer you to be tempted above that ye are able; but will with the temptation also make a way to escape, that ye may be able to bear it. (KJV)

You're already a winner before your next temptation, and that's some seriously good news for the coming week!

Prayer

God my Father, there are so many voices of defeat and discouragement that say a man cannot walk in faithfulness to You and his wife. Please drown out these lies with Your truth. Lord, I know You are calling me to walk in consistent faithfulness and purity and that You also empower me by the Spirit that indwells me. I desire to live in total faithfulness before You and my wife. When temptations come, remind me of the truth of Your Word that says I'm never a victim and that You have provided a way of escape—the path of triumph for me in every situation. Thank You for the victory You have provided through Your Son. In Jesus's name, amen.

47

Comfort

Blessed be the God and Father of our Lord Jesus Christ, the Father of mercies and God of all comfort, who comforts us in all our tribulation, that we may be able to comfort those who are in any trouble, with the comfort with which we ourselves are comforted by God.

2 Corinthians 1:3–4 NKJV

When a new child arrives with limitations, or a disease overtakes a loved one, or an accident alters the life we'd hoped for, or we are betrayed by those close to us, it's almost as if life itself was designed to create in us the need to be comforted.

Of this you can be certain: Whether it happens today or tomorrow, life will teach you your need for God's comforting hand.

In the midst of your need, how will you lead? What will be the message your life speaks to your wife about the presence and goodness of God when life spreads adversity and trauma over your day? As it is with any sport, so it is with faith: *You play how you practice.*

In marriage, the storms of life don't build your faith. They put the faith you already have on display for your wife to see and experience.

If they haven't already arrived, troubled times are sure to come. Jesus said in John 16:33, "These things I have spoken to you, that in Me you may have peace. In the world you will have tribulation; but be of good cheer, I have overcome the world" (NKJV).

What happens in your spirit when you're hit with the unexpected? Your theology—what you actually believe—is revealed. Only in the valley of adversity, when our words of praise are put to the test, do we live out the faith we have.

It's under pressure that our true level of maturity and walk with God emerge. Have you felt the brutal hand of this fallen world rip from your grasp a hope, a dream, a person? Has God allowed something you love to be crushed?

You serve a God who knows what loss is. You serve a High Priest who has lived the trauma that has touched you. He knows, and when pain is blinding you from seeing the path forward, He will comfort you if you will let Him. Will you receive the comfort God offers through the Holy Spirit?

You have needed or will need the comfort of your Father, who knows your journey and is ready and eager to provide it for you. But what could possibly be the purpose in the pain He allows you to go through? *Why* is an understandable question.

And there is an answer: You can never offer to someone else—to your wife—what you haven't received from the Father. And what you have received is to be used for God's blessing in your wife's life. God gave you His Holy Spirit, the Comforter, so when the worst life has to offer pays your wife an unwelcome visit and plunges her into a deep valley of loss and pain where light can't penetrate, you can comfort her and be the minister of His grace to her heart.

Reflection

- Am I willing to receive the Father's comfort should life hand me the unthinkable?
- Have I settled in my mind the goodness of God regardless of the badness of my circumstances?
- With my current level of faith and maturity, how would I lead my wife through a painful, heart-crushing experience?

Application

There are no shortcuts through pain, but there's no impediment to God's comfort except your willingness to receive it. The comfort God gives comes when you choose to base your perspective on what He says rather than on how circumstances have made you feel.

Remember, you can only give what you have received. Will you let your Father comfort you in pain?

Remind yourself that God's comfort is for you to share with your wife. Prepare your heart and mind to be attuned to your wife's need for comfort.

Prayer

God my Father, thank You that You are a Father who will be there with me when life brings pain, when I need the comfort a son can only know from his Father's supporting hug. You are there for me. I believe that. Thank You. I don't want my faith to be just words, some theory that's easy to say but far from the reality of who I really am. Lord, I want faith that is real, strong, and unwavering on the journey of my life with You. I say again, along with the man whose son Your Son healed, "Lord, I believe; help my unbelief" (Mark 9:24 NKJV). Father God, may I listen to Your words of truth so I can receive the comfort I need that You so readily offer. Your Word is clear—the pain I experience and the comfort You give are to equip me to comfort others, starting with my wife when she is in need. Lord, may I receive so I am prepared to give. In Jesus's name, amen.

48

Rest

And he said unto them, Come ye yourselves apart into a desert place, and rest a while: for there were many coming and going, and they had no leisure so much as to eat.

Mark 6:31 KJV

Have you and your wife been running hard? Do you fall into bed at night exhausted? Do you have that creeping sense of running on fumes, only to hear the alarm clock about two hours before you wanted to? That's a pretty typical life in the twenty-first century as we try to stuff thirty-six hours' worth of activity into our twenty-four-hour day. Jesus and the disciples faced the same problem.

Most people regarded Jesus as a very good leader—especially His spiritual enemies. They were so convinced of His effectiveness, they tried several times to kill Him. Even though Jesus was effective and busy, He made sure that He and His disciples didn't run on empty. When it came to downtime, Jesus showed remarkably consistent leadership.

The man who did more than anyone to turn the world upside down made it a priority to get away from the demands of His life and rest. But He did more than that. As a leader of others, He made sure that His disciples got time away too. And for what?

For leisure. Every self-help or business book about maximum productivity and effectiveness has a section on the necessity of inner rejuvenation and rest, but all the business gurus are two thousand years late to the game. Jesus had this practice well in hand.

"Time off" doesn't have much of a spiritual ring to it, but Jesus ensured that this was a regular part of His life and the lives of His disciples. Taking care of the needs of those who are looking to you for setting the pace in your home is real spiritual leadership.

If Jesus needed regular time to recharge and taught His disciples that same discipline, you need rest too. And if you're one of those husbands who feel guilty for taking time out of your work schedule to rest, you're going to have to put those feelings in their place. Is it time for a change in your habits?

Jesus not only led by example but also protected those He led by making sure they, too, got the downtime they needed. Are you protecting your wife's need for rest? It's not an extravagance to indulge in but a necessity to protect. If you are caring for the need you both have for rejuvenating rest away from the regular demands of a busy life, you're caring for yourself and her like Jesus cared for those He was responsible for. If not, it is time for a change.

Reflection

- What is my perspective on taking regular times of rest?
- Do I look at times away from routine as necessary or as unjustifiable interruptions to important routines?
- Am I resting weekly, or is Sunday just another day stuffed with activity?
- When do I actually rest?
- Have I been confusing one big vacation with regular times of rest?
- Do I ensure that my wife is taking the downtime she needs to be refreshed?

Application

- Make sure you are meeting regularly with the Lord in the mornings (or at night . . . but morning sets the tone for your day).
- Check in with your wife on her morning routine. Ask if there is a positive change you can make that will enable her to have devotional time in the morning too.
- Take time to rest each week, as God intended.
- Purpose to be aware of when you and your wife are becoming run down from all you do, and in the coming month when you see that one or both of you are needing a time of rejuvenation, make it happen!

Prayer

God my Father, the idea of resting almost makes me feel guilty. Yet I know that rest is necessary, and Your Word could hardly be clearer. You want me to rest . . . and You want my wife to rest. Help me to listen to Your voice on this matter in the coming week. Help me to see that rest is Your blessing on our lives and that we are made to rest—to come away from the busyness of our regular lives to receive what we need from You. Help me, Lord, to get better at this priority in my life and marriage. In Jesus's name, amen.

49

Mercy

For judgment is without mercy to the one who has shown no mercy. Mercy triumphs over judgment.

James 2:13 NKJV

Most people are good at spotting in others what they are most familiar with in themselves. How naturally we take to the role of judge and jury when we see our own faults in others.

Marriage affords many opportunities for judging your wife. It's not that she isn't a wonderful person, but living life together means that at some point, she will do or say something that is different from what you want her to. On top of that, there are the genuine miscalculations, blunders, wrong choices, and mistakes in judgment. A car accident that shouldn't have happened, for instance, or a thousand other things.

Of course, you do the things in all these categories too, but that's different, right? Or is it?

This is the point Jesus wanted Peter and His other followers (and their husbands!) to understand from the parable He told about a servant who owed more than he could ever pay back (Matt. 18:21–35).

Peter asked Jesus how often he should forgive the same person. Jesus answered with a story about a servant who was threatened with prison because he couldn't pay what he owed—ten thousand talents (the money of that day). This man owed more than he would have been able to pay back from the wages of many lifetimes.

Facing prison, the servant begged for mercy, claiming (impossibly) that he'd pay back everything. But to pay back even one talent would have taken over sixteen years. The master knew he could never pay what he owed and, considering his pitiful cry for more time, chose to have mercy on his servant, forgiving him the entire debt. His burden was lifted. In an instant, he was completely free.

Soon after, the man who had received so great a gift of mercy found one of his fellow servants who owed him what amounted to about four months' wages. As the man had done before his master, this servant begged for mercy and time to pay. Instead of showing mercy, as he had received, the man had his fellow servant thrown in prison.

When the master heard that his servant showed no mercy for so small a debt after he had been forgiven so much, he had him brought in and said,

> You wicked servant! I forgave you all that debt because you begged me. Should you not also have had compassion on your fellow servant, just as I had pity on you? (18:32–33 NKJV)

The master was furious and delivered that unmerciful servant to be tortured until he could pay everything he owed. It's hard to pay back a debt when you're in prison being tortured.

Jesus ends His teaching by saying God the Father will not forgive those who don't forgive. It's not unclear or hard to understand, and the implications are ominous.

Where would you be without the mercy God has shown you regarding the debt you have no capacity to pay? You don't have to guess. God desires that you, having received the complete cancellation of your debt of guilt, remember how much you've been forgiven and likewise show your wife the beautiful grace and mercy you have been given.

Mercy is the default response of the husband who doesn't lose sight of how much God has forgiven him.

Reflection

- Do I have a merciful spirit toward my wife when something goes wrong? Or do I communicate judgment and condemnation?
- How would she describe her experience in these moments?
- Do I make her feel that I'm quick to judge her while overlooking or ignoring my own mistakes?
- Have I truly taken to heart God's warning to those who are unmerciful?

Application

Establish a time to meet with your wife when you won't be interrupted, and ask her, with a humble spirit, how you make her feel when she makes a mistake.

Meditate on the truth that God has declared regarding the end of the person who doesn't show mercy.

Prayer

God my Father, I desire to grow and mature in this matter of extending mercy to my wife. I know this is Your desire for me, and You made it very clear in Matthew 18: You have forgiven me a debt I could never repay—thank You, Lord! But when I'm dealing with my wife, You expect me to keep in mind what You have done for me so that I will have the same merciful spirit toward her should there ever be a reason. If I ever feel the "judge" rise in my heart again when dealing with my wife, please quickly remind me that I do the same things, or other things that are equally in need of mercy, and that You simply will not tolerate an unmerciful spirit. Lord, You have forgiven me so much. Fill me with Your spirit of mercy toward others, starting with my wife. In Jesus's name, amen.

50

Self-Control

For God gave us a spirit not of fear but of power and love and self-control.

2 Timothy 1:7 ESV

When the Bible speaks of the fruit of the Spirit, the first thing we should get clear in our minds is what that phrase means. If we're not careful, it will remain a vague, undefined spiritual concept without real meaning and daily application to our lives—just the way your spiritual Enemy wants it.

The fruit of the Spirit is the resulting transformation of a renewed mind and godly character when a person is *presently* in communion with the Father. It's why Jesus Christ came—that you might be reconciled to (in fellowship with) God the Father. And what does this look like in your daily life? Prayer, reading His Word, worshiping Him, and remaining in close communication with Him throughout your day.

Once you belong to God through repentance, having received the free gift of His saving grace through faith in Jesus Christ's payment for your sins, and are consequently indwelt by the Holy Spirit, the responsibility for such closeness and intimate communion with the Father is yours, not God's. This surprising truth is discovered in James 4:8, "Draw near to God, and he will draw near to you" (ESV).

The result of this communion with the Father is the fruit of the Spirit in your life and relationships. It's why we are told to "pray without ceasing" (1 Thess. 5:17)—to remain in communion and fellowship with the Father at all times throughout our day.

The evidence—the fruit—of this close fellowship in your life is that you will have self-control, another concept that requires clarity and understanding. When we think of self-control, we typically think of not flying off the handle or of controlling our emotions—unlike the man ahead of me in line once at the airline ticket counter. Not a single foul curse word was left unused as he spewed his venom at the agent for the disruption to his flight. When he raged away, I was next and began with an apology for what she had just been subject to. "Don't worry about me," she said cheerfully. "He's going to Los Angeles; his bags are going to Miami."

Self-control isn't just a benefit in your marriage (or at the airport!); it's the evidence that you are maturing as a husband. And the particular self-control spoken of here isn't just about governing your temper when things anger you. This specific manifestation of the Spirit in your life is speaking to your bodily appetites, particularly your sensual appetites.

A husband who claims to be Christian and in the same breath claims that he can't stop looking at other women or watching porn or fantasizing about sexual encounters with another person is a husband who is speaking of the absence of the Spirit in his life. Let's not forget we are speaking of the Holy Spirit—the Spirit that raised Jesus Christ from the dead (Rom. 8:11). When it comes to your self-control, He's up to the task.

If you have this kind of self-control, you are a blessing to your wife's heart. If you lack self-control, the resolution of this deficit is not difficult. Draw near to God—and remain near to Him—in this moment, in this day, and every day.

The only Christian the Holy Spirit doesn't convict of sin is the person who has allowed his heart to grow cold. When you remain in communication with the Father throughout your day, the Spirit will convict you of the change God desires to see in your life. When you walk in the Spirit, self-control is the natural result.

Reflection

- Have I lived with a lack of self-control in my life that the Holy Spirit is prompting me to face?
- When it comes to the appetites of my flesh, where am I particularly vulnerable?

Application

- Make a list of the areas in which you demonstrate a lack of self-control. Name them and bring them before the Lord, asking for His transformation in these areas of your life.
- Today and every day this week, focus on walking with God, being in fellowship and communication with Him at all times throughout your day.
- Ask your wife to pray for you, that you will listen to the Spirit's promptings and be protected against the Enemy's intentions for you.

Prayer

God my Father, there is no growth and no maturity without remaining in communion with You. Lord, I desire to grow. I desire to walk as the godly husband You have called me to be. I desire to be a blessing to my wife. Lord, I've read Your words in the Bible, and I understand what You are saying about self-control in my life. Now burn Your truth into my soul that it should be my first thought as I encounter the opportunities for self-control in the coming days of walking in fellowship with You and my wife. In Jesus's name, amen.

51

Perseverance

And let us not be weary in well doing: for in due season we shall reap, if we faint not.

Galatians 6:9 KJV

Perseverance is like a muscle. The more it is exercised, the stronger it gets. God calls you to develop that muscle, to grow in your capacity to persevere, because strength is going to be needed for what lies ahead.

When it came to perseverance, the apostle Paul was a rock. He was incarcerated multiple times and faced death often. If you were thrown into prison because of your witness for Jesus Christ, would you persevere in confident faith with a positive attitude, ready to sing praises to God?

Five different times, Paul was given thirty-nine lashes because of the opposition of the Jewish leadership to his witness for

Christ. Why thirty-nine? Because the beating was so severe, it was said that forty lashes would kill a man. Would you be willing to be beaten almost to death multiple times for the witness of Jesus Christ and still persevere in what God had called you to do?

Three other times, Paul was beaten with a rod by the Romans. One time Paul was stoned. Thinking they had killed him, the crowd left him for dead. Three different times he was shipwrecked.

Yes, Paul had his mettle tested, but he had perseverance. Life will test yours too if you're faithful. Jesus guarantees it when He tells us that the world hated Him; they will hate us too (John 15:18).

Perseverance comes from resting in the power of the Holy Spirit, which brings a mental toughness that allows you to focus on your destiny in Christ and the promises of God, regardless of the chaos of the present storm that engulfs you. It's that kind of perseverance that God is inviting you to develop—to choose. Why? Because He knows you're going to need it. And your wife is going to need that strength in you.

Speaking through the writer of Hebrews, the Holy Spirit says, "*For ye have need of patience*, that, after ye have done the will of God, ye might receive the promise" (Heb. 10:36 KJV).

Not only does a man who perseveres not complain about hardship, he chooses a good attitude in bad circumstances and refuses to quit. He refuses to throw in the towel. He will not despair and turn his back on God. Perseverance is holding on to confidence in God's purpose in the face of confusion or pain, without demanding to understand.

Perseverance makes you effective and faithful in the face of opposition and hardship. Much of what life dishes up, you would never choose for yourself. And, like most, you don't know the extremes of what you are capable of. But God does, and He's calling you (or will soon) to persevere and choose confidence in Him. That inner strength will be a blessing to your wife, bringing a spirit of peace to your life, your home, and your marriage.

Reflection

- Am I committed to persevering when opposition arises, or am I inclined to shrink back from being a bold witness?
- Am I protecting my family with confident, persevering faith, or do I cultivate a spirit of fear in my wife and in my home by how I speak of our place in this increasingly hostile world?
- What does my wife see in me?

Application

- The beginning of cultivating a spirit of perseverance is to establish a proper thinking pattern about even the smallest things. Ask yourself, "How should I respond the next time something goes wrong?"
- Purpose to persevere with a positive attitude and countenance when you encounter hardship.
- Remind yourself that your Father God is with you, has a plan, and remains in control, regardless of circumstances.

Prayer

God my Father, You desire perseverance in me. I invite You to do Your work in my heart as You seek to conform me to the image of Christ, who went willingly to the cross—persevering through the humiliation, torture, and pain. I know You're looking for growth and maturity in me. May I listen to Your Holy Spirit's voice as You put me in the refining fires of life. May I be found trustworthy to persevere when called on by You. In Jesus's name, amen.

52

Gospel

For I am not ashamed of the gospel of Christ: for it is the power of God unto salvation to every one that believeth; to the Jew first, and also to the Greek.

Romans 1:16 KJV

K ing David had had many successes against his enemies, but Bethlehem, the king's hometown, was still in enemy hands, a garrison of the Philistines. One day, David said to no one in particular, "Oh that one would give me drink of the water of the well of Bethlehem, which is by the gate" (2 Samuel 23:15 KJV). It wasn't a command. It wasn't a requirement. It was a comment from the longing of his heart. While the king's desire was directed at no one, it was overheard by some men.

Three of David's mighty warriors purposed to satisfy the longing of their king. *He must have a drink from that well!* they decided among themselves.

As a garrison, the town of Bethlehem was heavily guarded, guaranteeing a high-risk venture for these men, but compared to the desire of their king, the risk to their lives was counted by them as nothing. They broke through enemy lines, drew water from the well, and returned to present it to King David. That is devotion.

As a Christian husband, you wouldn't hesitate to say you are a follower of Jesus Christ, but is that devotion on His terms or yours? Every man is inspired by the story of David's mighty men, but what happens when your life rests in the balance between safety and following the desires of your King? Jesus has not been unclear about what He expects His disciples to do.

> All power is given unto me in heaven and in earth. Go ye therefore, and teach all nations, baptizing them in the name of the Father, and of the Son, and of the Holy Ghost: Teaching them to observe all things whatsoever I have commanded you: and, lo, I am with you always, even unto the end of the world. (Matt. 28:18–20 KJV)

And in John 14:15, Jesus says, "If you love Me, you will keep My commandments" (NASB). David's mighty men had only to overhear the desire of their king to spring into action. You have the very words of Christ speaking His expectation directly to His disciples. Are you His disciple? To lead your marriage as a Christian husband is to make sure you and your wife prioritize the message Christ has given you to speak together to the world.

No one will listen very long to a hypocrite. If the truth of the gospel isn't seen and experienced in the love of your marriage, there is no power in you to speak on behalf of the gospel of Jesus Christ—your nonverbal testimony is saying something different from what God wants people to see about Him in your marriage.

The gospel is the power of God leading to salvation. And when that transforming power is unleashed in your marriage, the beauty of God's love is seen by everyone who encounters you and your wife, giving you authenticity to speak boldly about God's free gift of grace offered through the sacrifice of Jesus to every person.

God is looking for couples who will boldly do His will in the same spirit as David's mighty men did for him. Are you and your wife hearing God's desire for you to serve His purposes in this world through your lives and marriage? Never forget, your marriage is what God is doing in the world.

Reflection

- Am I zealous for what Christ wants of me?
- Is my goal to please God with my life or to please myself, with a bit of God on the side?
- As a couple, do we declare the power of the gospel by how we live and by what we say?

Application

- Make a list with your wife of the ways your marriage speaks love and unity to others who know or encounter you.
- Make another list of anything that would detract from your testimony.
- Are you prepared to share the gospel with another person? If God brought someone to you who had never heard the gospel, could you show them what the Bible says about salvation through the death, burial, and resurrection of Jesus Christ?

Prayer

God my Father, my life is not my own. You have bought it with the blood of Jesus Christ. I have not been as bold for the gospel as I know You desire of me. Lord, fill my heart with boldness and the resolve to lead my wife in love. I pray that we will keep in the forefront of our minds that our marriage is for Your glory, to share with the world how Jesus loves the church, and that we will be ready to speak the truth of the gospel to people You bring into our lives. In Jesus's name, amen.

Closing Note

Friend, God bless you as you seek to live an obedient life of faith, honoring God and blessing your wife. I pray you will be inspired to remain in communion and fellowship with the Father every day, pursuing Him in prayer, praise, and worship. I pray you will keep reading the Word as a disciple of Jesus Christ and yielding your life to the instructions you find there. And I pray that your marriage will reflect the love that Jesus Christ has for His bride, the church, and that you receive and obey the instructions He gave the church in the Great Commission:

> Go ye therefore, and teach all nations, baptizing them in the name of the Father, and of the Son, and of the Holy Ghost: Teaching them to observe all things whatsoever I have commanded you: and, lo, I am with you always, even unto the end of the world. Amen. (Matt. 28:19–20 KJV)

The end of the world . . . it's coming! Look up, for your redemption draws near! In the meantime, may our loving heavenly Father find us to be loving, faithful men.

Matt Jacobson is a teaching elder/pastor of Cline Falls Bible Fellowship and the founder of FaithfulMan.com, an online social media community focusing on marriage, parenting, and biblical teaching. He is the creator of Freedom Course, teaching men the powerful, biblical path to getting completely free from porn and sexual sin (Freedom-Course.com). Matt is the author of the bestselling *100 Ways to Love Your Wife* and *100 Words of Affirmation Your Wife Needs to Hear*. He lives with his wife, Lisa, in the Pacific Northwest, where they have raised their eight children. Together Matt and Lisa are cohosts of the popular *Faithful Life* podcast.

Hands-On Advice
to *LOVE* Your Spouse Better

Simple, Powerful Action Steps to
Love Your Child Well

Connect with
MATT and **FAITHFUL MAN!**

FaithfulMan.com
BiblicalMarriageCoach.com

Cohost of the *FAITHFUL LIFE* Podcast

@FaithfulMan